"What is Truth?"

by

Rev. Ken D. Walston, Jr.

First Printing

© 2014 by Rev. Ken D. Walston, Jr.
All Rights Reserved

Second Printing

© 2022 by Rev. Ken D. Walston, Jr. (Revised)
All Rights Reserved

Third Printing

© 2025 by Rev. Ken D. Walston, Jr. (Revised)R2
All Rights Reserved

No part of this book may be reproduced, stored in a retrieval system or transmitted in any form or by any means without the prior written permission of the author and publisher, except by a reviewer who may quote brief passages in a review to be printed in a newspaper, magazine, or journal.

Any characters appearing in this work are substantiated.

Softcover ISBN: 978-0-578-62996-4

PUBLISHED BY

Ken-na Outreach Publication

www.kennaoutreach.org

Printed in the United States of America

This book is dedicated to

The Way, the Truth and the Life.
The One who sits at the Right Hand of the Power of God and will come again for His Church (all who believe in their hearts that He is Lord and God),
The Alpha and the Omega, the Beginning and the End,
The Only Begotten Son of God,

Yeshua of Nazareth
HaMashiach

FOREWORD

In our quest to find Truth, we question everything.

Before you know the Truth, you know nothing.

After you find the Truth, it becomes the accumulation of knowledge and growth in it.

Once you believe it to be the Truth, your faith sustains it.

Rev. Ken D. Walston, Jr. Evangelist
Executive Director of **Ken-na Outreach** ✡ ™ Ministries ©1995
Ordained Minister and Doctor of Divinity

CHAPTER I
(God speaks only the Truth)

In our language Truth is a noun (Person, Place or Thing); mostly regarded in conjecture with the substance of One's Being in equality and justice.

It resonates Sincerity, Fact and Accuracy.

From the human perspective, to speak the Truth means that you are testifying to unquestionable reality and actuality and to judge the Truth would equate that you are accurate beyond a "Reasonable Doubt" in what you are testifying.

Truth is Supreme and Divine by nature; it is the standard by which all justice prevails in righteousness.

It is the absolute Nature of God and transcends any positive human affirmation of that which sustains goodness.

There is no middle ground or gray area within the Truth.

Anything other than the Truth is a Lie. Truth is a stand-alone and Eternal Entity.

In the Abode and Presence of God, which some call Heaven and others call Paradise, Truth abides in every aspect of Substance and Being, there it is Eternal, Pure and Powerful.

It is where Debate ends and all Doubt subsides, where the Absolute combines with Infinity and Eternity and is the course of an Endless Day.

There is no Doubt to the Truth, it transcends above every perpetrating prejudice or human seneschal and becomes the essence of a single Divinity.

If Justice was the precept behind what Truth is, then there would be no canonical means of verification to absolution.

Justice under human concept invokes a determination of finding the Truth under the pretense of the Law, which seeks mitigation in order to conclude or compromise a ruling, which is most often flawed by inherent prejudice (sin nature) in the collection and presentation of evidence to concede that the facts are accurate and without the factor of a reasonable doubt.

Finding the Truth from the human scheme of things through a so-called Justice System under the law, means that there are two sides, a plaintiff and a defendant, in which one is already the guilty party but is being hidden from both the judge and or a jury. It must be proven by human interaction, argument and evidence through representatives (Attorney's / Lawyers), who must by law do their best to prove that their side is innocent, whether it is true or not. So, in many cases, the guilty may be found not guilty and go free and the reverse can be true where the innocent may be found guilty and face punishment under the law even to the extent of imposing death.

The notion that Justice reveals the Truth through the process of the Law is falsely narcissistic and shows how distant we are from the order in which God derives what Truth is.

The Law was given by God to man in order to show how sinful the true nature of man really is and how difficult it would be for man to obtain righteous standing in the Presence of Absolute Holiness and Truth.

The Law does nothing but hold each and every one of us accountable to our inherent Sin Nature and constant abilities to break the statutes of the Law and become Law Breakers (Criminals) because of the imposing edicts according to the Law.

The fact that an oath must be taken in order to hold an individual accountable to the Truth when giving a testimony, which then becomes under the Law a "Sworn Testimony" so that such a breech becomes a violation of Perjury, shows how sinister the Law characterizes our human systemic sin nature.

No matter how good you try to be or how honest and forthright your actions may be in going about your daily life, the Law is a constant overlord which insights prejudice and judges everything we do.

There is no reward under the Law, only the accepted compliance which is expected of you with it, but notwithstanding, there is punishment and condemnation if you cannot meet the "Letter Of" or the interpretive context of the Law. According to the Law, if broken or violated, you must be held accountable and bound to its power and authority. You are seen by its edicts as a Law Breaker.

Grace, Mercy and Forgiveness are not virtues which the Law expounds or perceives under its jurisdiction.

Therefore, Justice is the outcome of Judgment and not the Law.

The Law addresses the condition of sin and the events of lawlessness but cannot pass Judgment.

The Law stands as witness of the sin and lawlessness and will be used as the standard by which judgment passes the measure of punishment according to the statutes prescribed within it.

Human justice is flawed in rendering a completely righteous verdict because of the influence of sin by the one who is acting as the judge; therefore, the truth cannot be completely revealed which would influence the action taken without impartiality in order to prescribe a perfect and righteous measure of punishment.

In order to have perfect judgment, the One who is acting as judge would also have to be perfect, so that no appeal could ever be filed against the judgment rendered and that the judgment would stand on the merit of its authority without the law.

Our difficulty as Human Beings has been with our struggle to obtain perfection under the Law. This, of course, was not the intent behind God giving the Law.

It was given to man under a shroud of mystery and could never be the hope of salvation that would redeem man from his sin, thus giving us perfection with God.

So, under the perspective of what Truth is, it is not the Law, for the Law only condemns and enlightens the nature and action of God's displeasure with man because of sin, but at the same time gives man a temporary way out from total destruction by a Holy God who cannot allow sin to stand in His Presence.

The buffer zone was Israel and that nation He would bring forth and a Priestly Tribe of chosen people to establish His Covenant of Eternal Salvation for all of the nations and peoples of the Earth.

God's Truth regarding Man's perfection would not be through the Levitical Priesthood or the Mosaic Law for this would at best only maintain temporary appeasement of God's Wrath and Holy Judgment, but would come about through the Eternal Covenant that He had made with Abraham, Isaac and Jacob (Israel); and through one of the Twelve Tribes that would come out of Israel (Judah).

It would only come by means of Grace through the Spirit of God the Father, YaHaVah (YAHWEH) proclaiming the Way, the Truth and the Life out of the Covenant He had made with His chosen Nation, who would bring forth the Savior of the World, the Only Begotten Son of God, Yeshua HaMashiach (Jesus the Messiah).

Under the pretense that Truth is Divine and not Secular, there is no argument that there is only One Truth, just as there is only One God.

Any diverse speculation which is created by the human element, gives way to Fact which is obtained through Wisdom as appropriated by God.

Notwithstanding, if Truth is based on a secular perspective, then it is tainted by a variety of different views and equations obtained through human intellectual and interactive knowledge (ideologies and philosophies) and will have possibly many gods (deity) and the division of many religions and cult factions arise with no absolute conjecture.

The manner in which this occurs gives way to human cultural segregation, diversity and tribal warring.

The major difference between monotheism and secular divinity or atheistic humanism is having one source of Truth and Divine Intervention.

Judaism, Christianity, and Islam all hold to the One God concept and all view God as the Creator of the Universe and to be a Holy Divine Being, all Powerful, all Knowing and with no beginning and no end.

*　　　*　　　*　　　*　　　*　　　*

Judaism and Christianity share the same root branch with Israel and the God of Abraham, Isaac, and Jacob as their source of Divinity. God made a solemn promise to Abraham that Sarah (his wife) would bare him a son (Isaac) and that child would be the heir to God's Covenant forever and a nation (Israel) would be born out of him that would be the chosen people of God everlasting. [The events of this truth are found in the TANAKH, Genesis 17:7-22]

Through this lineage God would redeem all mankind back unto Himself through a Messiah (God's Anointed One - the God Man).

The intersection where Judaism and Christianity part ways is with the Christian declaration of Faith that the coming Messiah has already come, as the Son of God - Yeshua HaNotzri (Jesus of Nazareth).

Christians believe that all of the prophetic references in the Holy Scriptures by means of the Torah and the writings of the Jewish Prophets and the Psalms about the Messiah were fulfilled by Yeshua at the time of His visitation.

His death, which was totally witnessed by hundreds of individuals and fully documented by both Jews and Romans.

His Resurrection to life by God the Father, which afterwards He appeared to more than five hundred people (1 Corinthians 15:6) in the course of 40 days, is the account of fulfillment to His Deity as the Son of God and as Messiah in His ability and authority in the forgiveness of sin for all mankind and the promise of our resurrection and Eternal Life through Him (John 11:25).

His Ascension into Heaven, witnessed by His Apostles and many others amongst them (Acts 1:6-11), where He is now seated at the Right Hand of the Power of God, makes Him One with Father God and the Spirit given to those who have been Born Again by way of their Faith, gives testimony to the Trinity of God as Father, Son and Holy Spirit being One in the Same (ELOHIM), there is only One God (Deuteronomy 6:4 and John 10:30).

Judaism is still waiting for the Messiah to show up and for God to give fulfillment to the fathers and His promises to the children and defeat their enemies, restore the Nation, and establish His Kingdom on Earth forever.

They view the pronouncing of Yeshua as the Son of God as blasphemous and totally reject Yeshua as Mashiach or even nothing more than a false prophet.

For the Jew, religion is secular at best, since the Holy Temple in Jerusalem was sacked, desecrated and destroyed by the Romans in 70 AD, along with Jerusalem and the Jewish Nation was scattered throughout the earth for nearly two thousand years, forcing Israel to live amongst the Gentile Nations.

Since then, the practices as defined and delegated by the Law (Torah) and the required Rabbinical Teachings, sacrifices and rituals demanded by God to fulfill His Covenant standing with Israel has stopped.

Without the Holy Temple in Jerusalem there can be no true religious fulfillment for the Jews; the Law of Moses still stands as sanctified but cannot be fulfilled to its fruition by means of the order of its commands and intent.

Nevertheless, the restoration of the Jewish Nation in 1948 and the gathering of Jews throughout the world back to Israel and the recovery of Jerusalem as the Capitol with the Six Day War in 1967 definitely marks the End-Time Events of prophecy as noted by the Prophets Daniel, Isaiah and Jeremiah.

This will lead to the restoration of the third Holy Temple in Jerusalem and the total restoration of all the land that God promised to Abraham for Israel.

This means that Israel will have to take back the land they have already given up and restore the nation's boundaries to what God showed Abraham as the Promised Land in Genesis 15:18 and Joshua 1:4.

*　　　*　　　*　　　*　　　*　　　*

Islam and the Arab Nations share a divided root with the God of Abraham through a different source with Ishmael, the son begotten to Abraham through an Egyptian maidservant of his wife Sarah.

He was conceived out of sin, doubt and disobedience to the Promise that God had given to Abraham as His chosen lineage.

Even though Ishmael was the first child born to Abraham, he was illegitimate (not coming through Sarah, but through her maidservant Hagar) and he would not be the heir to God's promise. [The events of this truth are found in the TANAKH Genesis 21:9-13]

Nevertheless, God made out of him a great nation and a people that would live by the sword and oppose the Covenant that God made with Isaac and the nation of his descendants (Israel).

There are two factions that would eventually make up what the Muslim and Arab Nations along with Islam would develop into.

Isaac had two sons, (twins) and within the womb of their mother they struggled against each other.

As their mother cried out to the Lord God asking why this was happening, the Lord told her that within her were two rival nations being born and that the older son would serve his younger brother.

The first coming out of the womb (named Esau) had his brother (named Jacob) tightly holding onto his heel as they were born. [The events of this truth are found in the TANAKH Genesis 25:19-26]

As it was, Esau had the Rights of the First Born, which meant that the blessing of his father Isaac and all of the property and authority within his tribe belonged to him; but God had made it known to Rebecca (Isaac's wife) that God's favor was with Jacob and the Everlasting Covenant He had made with Abraham and Isaac would be passed down to Jacob and his lineage, not Esau.

It says that God Loved Jacob and Hated Esau (Malichi 1:3 and Romans 9:13)

Esau would sell his birth right of the First Born to his brother Jacob for a bowl of stew and Isaac would unswervingly give his Blessing to Jacob and pass the lineage of God's Everlasting Covenant through him. [These events are found in the 26th, 27th and 28th Chapters of the Book of Genesis]

Esau married foreign wives and separated from the traditions of his father Isaac and formed through his lineage what is today, the peoples of the surrounding Arab nations.

Jacob moved in the opposite direction from Esau and fulfilled God's Covenant by having twelve sons, which formed the Twelve Tribes of Israel and the Nation of God's choosing.

So, between Ishmael and Esau the Arab and Muslim nations have developed and through them has come the religion of Islam and with it the radical opposition to Israel.

As warring nations by origin and birth, their charter would be to never have peace with Israel but would develop and employ a posture of Jihad (Holy War) against the nation of God's chosen people.

Their declaration to all of the nations of the world would be utter hatred and demand for the death of every Jewish man, woman and child and complete the destruction of Israel by driving them into the sea and wiping them off the face of the earth.

This is the teaching of their holy book Koran (Qur'an) and the Sunnah. They pronounce the hatred of anything other than Islam and this one pinpoint expression of hatred is towards Israel and the call for its annihilation.

In Islam, their children are raised to hate Israel and every Jew by being taught that all Jews are the descendants of apes and pigs, which in their culture are the lowest and most defiled creatures on earth and are disposable without any care or compassion.

In Islam, anything not Islamic (Infidel) is defiled and must be either converted to Islam or eradicated (killed).

In Islam, living by the sword and dying by the sword for Jihad means assured entrance into Heaven and the rewards of a warrior of Allah; seventy-two virgins and all the alcohol you can consume.

Don't know what happens when the seventy-two virgins are no longer virgins, I guess they just keep replicating themselves over and over again for all of eternity.

I don't think the terrorists are considering that, all they care about is "The Prize!"

The god of Islam (Allah), even before Islam existed was referred to as the cult "Moon-god" and by the original name *SIN but* given the title as al-ilah *(the deity)* and later referred to by many other names such as Nanna, Suen and Asimbabbar.

His symbol was the crescent moon and was worshiped in ancient Syria, Persia, Canna, Egypt and by the Assyrians, Babylonians, and the Akkadians.

The word "Allah" comes from the compound Arabic word Al "the" and ilah Arabic for "god" (the god).

Their Prophet Muhammad (Born 571AD – Died 632AD) was raised in the religion of the Moon-god (Allah) and within his culture as they worshiped more than 360 different gods and goddesses (pagan idols), Allah was considered as the chief deity in the dominant cult of his time.

In pre-Islamic times the pagan Arabs even used Allah in the names they gave to their children. Both Muhammad's father and uncle had Allah as part of their names.

The fact that they were given such names by their pagan parents proves that Allah was the title for the Moon-God cult even in Muhammad's day.

In stark contrast, the TANAKH (Old Testament) of the Judeo-Christian Holy Bible rebuked the worship of the Moon-God as a cult and abomination to the Most High God (Deuteronomy 4:16-19; 17:3; II Kings 23:5; Jeremiah 8:2-3; 19:13; Zephaniah 1:5 as a few examples).

The first and most Holy of all the Commandments given through the Law of Moses and the Torah is, "*to have no other gods before me...create and worship no idols or graven image*" (Exodus 20:3-5); and to love the Lord your God, with all of your heart, with all of your mind and with all of your being and to have no other gods before me, thus says the Lord God (ADONAI).

It was Muhammad who after declaring himself as "The Prophet of God", decided that Allah was the highest deity of the other gods, and all Muslims and Islam would recognize and worship Allah as the only god. Legend declares that Muhammad received insights and messages from the Angel Gabriel over a period of 23 years which became their holy book (Qur'an). Muhammad did not write the Qur'an himself, but recited the revelations, which were then memorized and written down by his companions. After Muhammad's death, these written and memorized fragments were compiled into the book which is known as the Qur'an today.

The issue with this is that unlike the God of the Hebrews (*YAHWEH*), this god Allah never proclaimed himself to any man as being God, other than given as a proclamation by Muhammad.

He was self-proclaimed by man to be God, whereas the God of Israel appeared to man and proclaimed Himself to be the Most High God and that there is no other gods above or before Him to be worshipped.

If this deity was and is still looked upon as the highest of all gods in Muslim Islam, then why is Allah never defined in the Qur'an?

Under Muslim Islam, Allah is a vengeful warrior, ready to smite and quick to demand the killing of the enemies of Islam (anyone not a Muslim or practicing Islam), the call for Jihad.

There is no love with this deity only strict obedience to the letter of the Qur'an or teaching of the Sunnah and worship through Islam.

There is no salvation from sin with the god of Islam, but rather sin is part of the edict of this religion.

Muslims cannot characterize what God is nor are they expected to visualize what God is.

There is no identity to Allah as a Father image and no kinship with his followers as children, but rather the opposite as a tyrannical race of bastards whose religion and worship calls for the murder, execution, and extinction of the human race outside of Islam all in the name of Allah.

One thing is for sure, no one is strapping a bomb to their bodies and blowing themselves up and murdering masses of people or beheading innocent people (including children) in the name of Yeshua (Jesus), but they are in the name of Allah and Islam!

In these times, not every Muslim (yet) is a terrorist, but every terrorist in the Middle East and around the world who is part of Islam is a Muslim.

It (Islam) is not a peaceful religion, and Muslims do not have a charter of peace or compassion for mankind outside of Islam if they follow the Qur'an but have very deep-rooted radical offshoots which are very oppressive and sinister.

The meaning of the word Islam is "Submission", the edict is clear and precise, world domination through the sword (Force) and slavery or death to anyone not able to be converted.

A true Muslim who follows the Qur'an as their holy book and lives their life under the rule of laws as associated to this book and religion must hate the nation and people of Israel (Jews) and fight against anyone who will not accept Islam as their true form of religion.

It is a fight to the death (what they call holy Jihad) and totally justified by their holy book, their religious leaders and their defiled religious doctrine.

They have no tolerance or compassion for anyone but their own kind and if you dare say a single disparity or have a negative opinion about their religion or their Prophet, then it is death to you and their outward display of hatred is beyond belief.

There is No Forgiveness in Islam regarding their fixation.

The fact that people individually would have hate in their hearts and attempt heinous acts like murder or other disparities is irrelevant in comparison to the teaching and practice of having the right to do such things as part of a religious doctrine or national politics and it becomes the anthem of a world-wide religious movement.

It is amazing how deceived these people really are, by their own proclamation they acknowledge their primordial faith as notably through Adam, Noah, Abraham, Moses and Jesus, whom they consider prophets.

Imagine, Abraham (the father and Patriarch of the Hebrews and Jewish Nation), Moses (a Hebrew and Giver of the Law of the Hebrew Nation-Israel) and Jesus (a Jew and the Son of the Most High God-Messiah), being part of their primordial faith, what an oxymoron!

Judaism has a wonderful salutation which expresses a heartfelt thankfulness to the Creator for the greatest gift possible, l'chayim

חי (To Life), which is the preponderance of Chai (Living).

In stark contrast to this, Islam has a different expression of a heartfelt hatred and the greatest terror possible, Jihad (Take Life), which is their preponderance of evil.

Another stark contrast between the god of Islam and the Judeo-Christian God is the image of the Father (Aba or Abba) and who He calls His Children.

The god of Islam does not call anyone children, but rather they are warriors; where the God of Israel call them His Children, not bastards, but true sons and daughters.

God is Love and a God of Peace; and His Wish is that the human race, all people, receive Salvation and Everlasting Life, in Abundance, through Faith in the Son of God (**Yeshua HaMashiach**).

[John 3:16 - "*For God so loved the world, that He gave His only Begotten Son, so that anyone who believes in Him should not perish, but have Everlasting Life*"]

Islam does claim a Messiah or Mahdi as formed by a concept derived from Hazrat Mirza Ghulam Ahmad, the founder of the Ahmadiyya Muslim community.

In 1891, he claimed on the basis of Divine Revelation, that he was the Promised Messiah and Mahdi whose advent had been foretold by the Prophet Muhammad.

Nevertheless, he died and did not fulfill the promise revelation of the Mahdi.

The One Big aspect of the calling and return of the Mahdi would be through an all-out Muslim (Islamic) uprising that would give way to an all-out world war and through this the Mahdi would return to establish his reign and proclaim and convert the entire world as Muslim Islamic and rule forever.

This is exactly what that little Iranian big mouth Mahmoud Ahmadinejad was claiming he would accomplish before he was ousted as President of Iran in 2013.

His current counterpart Masoud Pezeshkian the new Iranian President, is a little bit more subtle and quiet with his sinister hatred towards Israel and ushering in the Mahdi, but the radical mindset is still the same and very real.

The bigger threat is not what the President of Iran says, but the edict of Iran's Supreme Leader, who at this moment in time is Ali Khamenei.

He's the one who is calling all the shots in Iran; it's a total Islamic religious dictatorship and the President is nothing more than a stooge for him.

He is undeniably anti-Semitic and calls for the complete and utter destruction of Israel and all Jews throughout the world.

Until recently (2025) Iran (Persia) was getting closer and closer to becoming a world Nuclear Superpower and Russia (The Bear) and most recently Turkey has become their biggest advocate in promoting it, but the current President of the United States of America, Donald J. Trump and the Prime Minister of Israel, Benjamin Netanayhu, put an abrupt stop to that..

Russia was throughout the 20th Century and now in the 21st Century the Major Proponent of every rogue nation and evil purpose derived throughout the world.

They were viewed as an **Evil Empire** way before President Ronald Reagan labeled them that back in the 1980s.

I personally believe that if Iran had gone nuclear, Russia and

Turkey would have aligned and join forces with them and their posture to dominate the Middle East would have been the biggest threat in modern history.

With this, it is very possible that North Korea having nuclear weapons could also have joined in with this alliance and began their own campaign to push forward with domination of their own region as they have been threatening to do.

At the other end of the Nuclear Spectrum is China (the Dragon) who is already flexing their military might and challenging the entire Region of Asia (The Kings of the East) and seeing how far they can go with intimidation and fear to bring it all under their submission.

Between these three evil factions will come the united forces for world domination that mankind has never witnessed before throughout all of history.

Bible Prophecy predicts these three powers (Persia, Russia, and China) as coming forth in the Last Days of the End-Times to annex world domination, as we are witnessing these events unfold right before our eyes.

As well, the stage has been set and will play out the fall of the greatest Superpower and advocate of Freedom and Liberty the world has ever known, the United States of America.

In order for world domination to take place, all opposition must be removed, and the United States is that biggest obstacle, but the powers of darkness and the evil presence that will dominate this world have an agent of collusion who is helping to remove that obstacle from within.

The Greatest Nation on the face of the earth will not be overthrown and neutralized by invading armies or forces from outside of the United States landing on our soil to invade and conquer; it is happening and will be implemented by subversion from within; by calling a lie the truth and the truth a lie.

Our own government has been our enemy! Our political and justice system is perverted and lawbreakers outwardly in the open.

The call for and acceptance of diversity is the poison that has divided us into warring groups within our society.

Lawlessness follows anarchy and anarchy flourishes in a divided society.

The current President of the United States, Donald J. Trump is without doubt, viewed by the large majority of Americans as an Anointed Leader given his position by God and is in and of himself, fulfilling many prophetic events in these Last Days of the End-Times.

In stark contrast, one of his predecessors, Barack Hussein Obama II, was a pronounced Muslim and radical extremist (an Anarchist) and has shown himself to be a traitor of both the Office of the Presidency and as Commander in Chief and in upholding the Constitution of the United States of America.

He was without doubt, the first Imperial President to ever hold the Office of Chief Executive of the United States and showed nothing but contempt and hatred towards the enforcement of the statutes of our Federation and the Rule of Law under the Constitution.

The push to move forward in the Impeachment of President Trump was a lavish and corrupt attempt to overrule the Will of the American People in appointing a duly elected Chief Executive and to replace him and substantiate an Anarchy and new formatted Constitution which fits into a Socialistic (Free-for-All) perverted form of government.

In the same way, Joesph Biden was a proxy for Obama in continuing his perverted agenda when he became President in

2021. It was an all-out attempt by the powers of darkness to overtake and destroy this nation and government once and for all.

The United States has always held the most promise of Freedom and Liberty for all of its citizens and throughout the world because of its inherent Judeo-Christian values and form of government, but it must be neutralized in order for this New World Order to dominate the entire world system, so that every nation and all peoples on this planet will conform to one authority, the ideals and power of one man, who will appear with the might and force of a Messiah or Mahdi.

This man will be able to deceive the entire world into believing that he is God-Like, and the promised Messiah and all worship and allegiance be given to him under the consequence of death (Revelation 13:11-14).

He begins his campaign under the banner of peace (World Peace) even achieving a Nobel Laureate, but within three and one-half years (42 months) reveals the true ruthless and demonic character that he really is.

He is a man that will be completely controlled by the Evil One. Satan will be cast down from the Heavenly Places and bound to the earthly realm, [Revelation 12: 7-9 - *Then war broke out in heaven. Michael and his angels fought against the dragon, and the dragon and his angels fought back. But he was not strong enough, and they lost their place in heaven. The great dragon was hurled down—that ancient serpent called the devil, or Satan, who leads the whole world astray. He was hurled to the earth, and his angels with him.*]

Once bound to the earth Satan brings forth his world leader (tyrant ruler) [Revelation 13:1 - *The dragon stood on the shore of the sea. And I saw a beast coming out of the sea. It had ten horns and seven heads, with ten crowns on its horns, and on each head a blasphemous name.]*

He will have supernatural powers given to him by the Evil One; [Revelation 13: 2b, 4 - *The dragon gave the beast his power and his throne and great authority… People worshiped the dragon because he had given authority to the beast, and they also worshiped the beast and asked, "Who is like the beast? Who can wage war against it?"]*

He will have charisma and a supernatural presence and the ability to make people believe a lie and denounce the truth.

The whole world will love his every word and follow him wherever he leads them. [Revelation 13: 5-8 - *The beast was given a mouth to utter proud words and blasphemies and to exercise its authority for forty-two months. It opened its mouth to blaspheme God, and to slander his name and his dwelling place and those who live in heaven. It was given power to wage war against God's holy people and to conquer them. And it was given authority over every tribe, people, language and nation. All inhabitants of the earth will worship the beast—all whose names have not been written in the Lamb's Book of life]*.

He will be a great proponent of "Peace" and will eventually broker a Peace Treaty between Israel and their enemies under a banner of his "New World Order".

He will introduce a System that will track and manage every human being on this planet and make them take a Mark of Allegiance to him in order to buy or sell anything. [Revelation 13: 14-18 - *Because of the signs it was given power to perform on behalf of the first beast, it deceived the inhabitants of the earth. It ordered them to set up an image in honor of the beast who was wounded by the sword and yet lived. The second beast was given power to give breath to the image of the first beast, so that the image could speak and cause all who refused to worship the image to be killed. It also forced all people, great and small, rich and poor, free and slave, to receive a mark on their right hands or on their foreheads, so that they could not buy or sell unless they had the mark, which is the name of the beast or the number of its name. This calls for wisdom. Let the person who has insight calculate the number of the beast, for it is the number of a man. That number is 666.]*

It is my Faithful and undoubting belief that we are living in the Last Days of the End-Times that Jesus described in the 24th Chapter of the Gospel of Matthew.

It is also my Faithful and unwavering belief that we are on the brink of the world events as described in the Book of Revelation and the introduction of the Man of Sin (Anti-Christ).

The only event left to happen on God's Prophetic Timetable, is the moving out of the Church of Laodicea Dispensational Period and into the beginning of the Tribulation Period, then the Taking Away of the Church (Body of Christ) out of this earth.

The Apostle Paul, under the guidance of the Holy Spirit prophesied this event, which has been labeled by the Christian Evangelical Movement as "The Rapture".

This event is mentioned by Paul twice, once to the Thessalonians and again to the Corinthians:

[1Thessalonians 4:15-17 - *According to the Lord's word, we tell you that we who are still alive, who are left until the coming of the Lord, will certainly not precede those who have fallen asleep (died). For the Lord himself will come down from heaven, with a loud command, with the voice of the archangel and with the trumpet call of God, and the dead in Christ will rise first. After that, we who are still alive and are left will be caught up together with them in the clouds to meet the Lord in the air. And so we will be with the Lord forever.]*

[1Corinthians 15:51-53 - *Listen, I tell you a mystery: We will not all sleep, but we will all be changed- in a flash, in the twinkling of an eye, at the last trumpet. For the trumpet will sound, the dead will be raised imperishable, and we will be changed. For the perishable must clothe itself with the imperishable, and the mortal with immortality.*]

This event will take place, but not in the way that it has been idealized by the modern evangelical movement since the early 20th Century. The Church of Laodicea, the last of seven (7) described periods of time in which the "Times of the Gentiles" would exist through the "Church Age" (Revelation 3:14-21), would be a Doubtful Church, a Wavering and Compromising Church, a point in the history of the Church that would become Lukewarm, as Yeshua described it, believing both the Truth and a Lie. Because of this (being neither Hot nor Cold), the Lord God (ADONAI) said that He would vomit them out of His Mouth.

Right now, in this current dispensation of time, we are this Church, and we will move into the beginnings of the Tribulation (Minor-3 ½ years) and (Major- 3 ½ years) and will experience the seven (7) Seal and Trumpet Judgements as described in the Book of Revelation Chapters 6 thru 11. Up until and when the Beast (Anti-Christ) sits in the Holy Place of the Third Temple and defiles the Temple (known as the Abomination of Desolation - Daniel 11:30-31, Matthew 24:15-16), will God take the Church out of this world (Rapture).

After this comes the Bowls of God's Wrath (Revelation 14:14-16) which we are promised by God that we (the Body of Christ) will not suffer His Wrath, for this will be a time like no other in the history of mankind or of this earth, that God will pour out His displeasure in the way of horrific Judgements.

I have witnessed a Word from the Lord God that we have already moved into the beginnings of the Minor Tribulation.

*   *   *   *   *   *

With the concepts and teachings of Judaism, God proclaims that all mankind (Humans) has sinned and fallen short of His Glory and that Atonement is available through His Covenant with Israel and keeping the Law of Moses.

Christianity proclaims that the fulfillment of God's Atonement and the redemption of mankind (each and every one of us) towards propitiation of sin has been given through Jesus of Nazareth, the Son of God and that through Him by an act of heartfelt Faith (without any doubt) we become the Children of God and have Eternal Life (no matter what race or religion you are).

That the Spirit of the Most High God (the Holy Spirit - Ruach HaKodesh) comes to the individual person who is repenting of their sins (sorry for their transgressions against God) and forgiveness is bestowed upon the repentant heart so that He transforms and lives in them, they are Born Again (John 3:3-8).

Now the Spirit of God has been given to mankind on the earth through the collection of Believers in Yeshua ADONAI (Jesus the Christ), known as the Church (Body of Christ).

This propitiation is based on God's Grace and His Love and Mercy through Yeshua as the Eternal Sacrifice and Saviour.

That mankind's abatement of sin is not possible through a religious order or the law, but only through the Atonement of the

Holy God to stand in proxy and give Clemency for all mankind and bridge the void between damnation and Eternal Life.

Yeshua openly proclaimed that, "*IAM (Ehyeh) the Truth, the Way and the Life; no one comes to the Father but through Me. If you had known Me, you would have known My Father (YaHaVah) also; from now on you know Him and have seen Him.*" (John 14:6-7)

Jesus was proclaiming His deity with God the Father as being one in the same, that He was God in Flesh on the earth and that God was presenting Himself to all of mankind in order that we all may receive forgiveness of sin and be reconciled to God (as His Children) once and forever. He was also proclaiming that the Holy Spirit (Ruach HaKosesh), which is the third part of the Godhead (ELOHIM), was also being given to all who proclaim their heartfelt faith in Him.

Not only as a nation of His Chosen People (Israel), but as His Body (the Church) who are imaged as a Bride and He as the Bridegroom [Revelation 19:6-7, 9 – *Then I heard what sounded like a great multitude, like the roar of rushing waters and like loud perils of thunder, shouting: "Hallelujah! For our Lord God Almighty reigns. Let us rejoice and be glad and give him glory! For the Wedding of the Lamb has come, and his bride has made herself ready... Then the angel said to me, "Write this: Blessed are those who are invited to the wedding supper of the Lamb!"*]

The Lamb described in this verse is Jesus (Yeshua ADONAI), the Lamb of God (the Eternal Sin Offering) and the great multitude and bride is the Church (Body of Christ).

The Truth is that there is only One God identified through the Covenant He made with Abraham, manifested through the Nation of His making (Israel) and sanctified by the appearance and visitation of the Anointed One (Messiah) to earth, born through the lineage of promise and prophecy from the House of David as the Word of God and became the Lamb of God (**Yeshua HaMashiach** – Jesus the Christ) who has taken away the sins of the world.

In order for God to save humanity, He had to become part of humanity and physically manifest Himself in the form of humanity (a Man - the God Man).

He (God) had to step out of Heaven not as a cosmic alien who would rule mankind, but by the order that God has created mankind and take on the form of the highest order of creation as the highest magnitude that a human could be formed (without sin).

That He would be conceived through a woman who was a virgin (in undefiled physical purity) and by the Holy Spirit (in complete physical and spiritual purity).

He took on the form of a human and with all of the physical attributes of a man, but without the inherent sin passed down by Adam (the first man) who brought sin upon all humanity due to disobedience and blasphemy.

The Son of God would be completely obedient to the Sovereign Will of God the Father (YAHWEH) and have the complete authority of God while physically on earth, including the authority to forgive sin.

It is as God stated, "*My Throne is in Heaven and My Footstool is the Earth*", and Yeshua bridged that gap.

Since the rebirth of the nation of Israel they have had to adapt to the reality that they are surrounded by enemies who want their complete and utter destruction with a proclamation and vow to push Israel into the sea so that they will be "No More".

When God made his original and Everlasting Covenant with

Abraham, he did so while Abraham was fatherless and had no children of his own yet. Thus, Abraham had to receive the promise from God by complete and total Faith.

God made it with the promise of a nation and the birth right of that nation to have a homeland.

God outlined the precise area that would be that birth right and promised it to the nation that would come from the union between Abraham and his wife Sarah, through their son Isaac and eventually his son Jacob (Israel) [The events of this truth are found in Genesis 15:7-21].

The land God gave to Israel includes everything from the Nile River in Egypt to Lebanon (south to north) and everything from the Mediterranean Sea to the Euphrates River (west to east).

All of the other tribes and peoples that surround this Promised Land that God gave to Abraham are the offspring of Ishmael and Esau and the warring nation(s) that would eventually become the enemies of the Nation that God would establish His Everlasting Covenant with.

God never promised to give any other tribe of people a Homeland or share of any land on the earth besides Israel.

God made only one Everlasting Covenant with Abraham and promise of a Chosen People that God would call His Own Children and that was through the lineage of Isaac and his son Jacob, who would sustain Israel.

With the Covenant came a solemn oath from God, "*I will Bless those that bless you; and I will Curse those that curse you*" [This truth comes from Genesis 12:3].

As this book is being written, at this very moment in time, Israel is under great attack by the surrounding nations of their ancestral enemies, in particular Iran.

They are once again fighting for their lives and right to exist as a Nation and Sovereign State.

They are under siege by terrorist organizations (like Hamas, the Muslim Brotherhood, ISIL) and countless others springing up almost daily, who are trying to destroy God's Chosen People through rocket attacks from the Gaza Strip and north from Lebanon; and by Suicide Bombers (Terrorist strapped with explosives on their bodies or in vehicles) coming into Tel Aviv and Jerusalem and trying to kill masses of people. All of these are proxies of Iran, who is the Head of the Snake.

There have formed many different Islamic Terrorist groups sparked by the call for Jihad and Intifada from Iran and Saudi Arabia creating uprisings in Syria, Iraq, Afghanistan, Egypt, Libya, the Sudan and throughout Northern Africa.

They are extremely ruthless and using barbaric tactics such as beheadings and crucifixion and mass executions by firing squads.

These savage Islamic murders are on an all-out campaign to make the entire Middle East one Islamic Nation under Sharia Law (also known as Qānūn-e Islāmī).

Iran has repeatedly called for that along with all Islamic forces to annihilate every Jew in the region and the Jewish State completely.

It also requires the driving out of any Infidel (non-Islamic Muslim) which includes Christians.

This persecution has started and is evident by the complete evacuation, mass killings and exile of the Christian community in the Iraqi city of Mosul in 2015, which has existed in both religious practice and habitation for the last sixteen hundred years. It is also spreading throughout Africa.

One theme that is consistent with this Islamic movement is that they hate everyone and anyone that is not Muslim Islamic to the point of complete annihilation.

It is happening now world-wide as this terror religion is spreading into every nation and executing their radical movement to persecute the Christian Church, as they see it being an ally rooted with Judaism and Israel.

The terrorists of this Jihad, has called upon each and every Muslim World-Wide to begin the killing and execution of all non-Muslims wherever they are encountered, meaning right in the streets of every city and neighborhood.

The BIG noticeable thing is the complicity of non-opposition to this call for murder by the Islamic / Muslim communities or religious leaders, because when it comes down to the Letter of the Law under the Qur'an, this is exactly what is called for, they're just doing what comes natural within their radical murderous religion and culture.

This hatred is not just political or tribal disputes of cultural indifference of human origin but are being enticed and led by spiritual forces at the highest level, demonic in character spurred on by the "Evil One" himself and the full force of the powers of darkness.

In the true cause of Righteousness, God has given us His Wisdom in acknowledging what we are really battling. [Ephesians 6:12 - "*for we fight not against flesh and blood, but against principalities, against powers, against the rulers of the darkness of this world, against spiritual wickedness in high places*"].

We are fighting against evil and battling forces that have supernatural (spiritual) power and authority in this world; but ADONAI has determined that Good shall prevail over evil and secured that on the Cross when He (Yeshua) died for all for the sins of this world and gave to us the victory over the powers of darkness and evil when God the Father raise Him from death, thus conquering death and sat Him at the Right Hand of the Power of God and secured our resurrection from death into Eternal Life through our Faith in Him.

This is what God has spoken through His Word and His Word is the Truth!

CHAPTER II
(God Reveals the Truth)

In our present dispensation we have become a global society, striving for unity in our human existence and achieving Peace under the coexistence as One Human Race devoid of any racial, political and religious prejudice; it's like asking a leopard to remove its spots or a porcupine to shed its hairy needles, it's not natural for either to do nor is it within the scheme of our sinful human nature to be without prejudice or not profile certain groups of individuals; but this is the direction of the New World Order in governance through the Unity of Political Correctness.

The historical problem with that agenda is that each and every one of us homo-sapiens are born with a "Free-Will" and separate individuality.

No matter how hard you try to make me think, act or conform to a single rule of social-political correctness and order of agenda, as a Free Man I may choose <u>not to</u> and in a Free Society individuals have the right <u>not to</u>.

The New World Order can only mean a One World Order that will rule as a united consortium of people with a single united mindset (political, social welfare and spiritual) and enforcement requiring a single governing Rule of Law and a single world-wide point of governance.

All perspectives of how the entire nations and peoples of the Earth will think, act and worship will have to be all One-in-the Same in order to comply with a single Rule of Law and governance. The New Global Society is a social and political propaganda which is forcing the entire world to embrace "Diversity" as the means of unification and striving for peace.

We are being encouraged and more and more expected (forced) to celebrate our ethnic and social diversities through the imposition of tyrannical laws in order to bring about acceptance of one another in unity and totally disregard our single and unique individualities for the sake of political correctness in a One World agenda to control each of us under the banner of Co-Existence and Peace.

As a Human Race, we never achieve utopian peace or transcending co-existence in the Fallen State that mankind currently resonates.

Separation within our specious society is caused by social and political prejudice, racial and cultural bigotries and abnormal psychological profiles of individual personalities that make it impossible for the Human Race to congeal into a united social order.

It's the direct result of our inherited separation from God because of sin; because of our first desire to rebel against God and pursue disobedience and thus become blasphemers.

When God created Man, He did so in a perfected State of Being and with the intention that the Human Race would worship Him with admiration and live in His Love and be sanctified Holy and Faultless.

Even if you don't believe in the "Creation" concept, then for sure we have evolved into this manner of separate individualities through the evidence of our human social disparities and desires for self-gratification and increased immorality.

The world is in a mess! And there will never be an end to it under human guise.

Mankind is not inherently good but has repeatedly demonstrated that our thoughts and actions are those of evil perpetuation against each other.

It's called our inherent Sin Nature, and it causes us to be imperfect, and it is also the reason we must all suffer death, which is the wages of sin. Sin is the "Death Gene".

We are all born as single entities, unattached from mother the moment the umbilical cord is severed.

It's interesting that as we come into this world, we are individuals, unattached and naked and that we die and leave in the same manner (as a metaphor).

Although in our genetic make-up we may resemble our mother's maternal factors or our father's paternal attitudes or vice-versa, we learn every aspect of our existence and behavior, the only instinctive human traits we all share are anatomic functions, and everything else about us is learned through the five senses of our anatomic being.

*   *   *   *   *   *

Finding the Truth as a complex order of divinity can only be spiritual confirmation.

In many cultures it's called searching for Enlightenment or Perfecting the Inner Being.

In our Modern English vernacular, it's called "Getting Religion".

The Enlightenment and Perfecting of the Inner Being process deals with the individual searching for reason and purpose of existence and determining the course of their life's journey in order to fit into a harmonious interaction with the world around them.

This kind of interactive reasoning with the elements of the physical environment (Earth or Cosmic Universe) and where the individual stands in relationship to them, can be self-fulfilling and temporal due to every changing attributes of the individuals' physical condition and the conditions of an ever-changing environment, which the individual may have no control over.

The true meaning of Life under this Chandra is always questionable and searching because the infinite vastness of the universe is uncomprehending to our finite minds.

One very popular yet pretentious Eastern Mystic form of transcendence is a practice called Transcendental Meditation or TM as it was popularized in the 1960s.

Introduced in India by the Maharishi Mahesh Yogi in the late 1950s, was not as much a religious expression as it was an environmental and health aid.

Even so, all forms of occultism have spiritual overtones and morph into a philosophical institution which ends up being related to a religious doctrine or dogma; and in many cases, such as TM, do not identify to a Divine Deity and relate only to secular humanism.

The practice of TM was to ease the human psyche and physical stress conditions of the human interactive experience through daily self-induced mantra meditation techniques.

This of course leads to psychological dependence and some degree of self-induced brainwashing.

The mantra could be as simple as humming at a resonated frequency that was pleasing to your ears or the internal emotion of what you were feeling (kind of like a self-hypnosis) or chanting a phrase or word over and over again to put you into a relaxed almost hypnotic state.

Because this kind of activity requires a degree of stamina with developing a repetitious chanting of the mantra (normally 1/2 hour to several hours) it produces a hyper-psychotic event and gestation of lowering the body's metabolic rate.

In many instances it is recommended that the beginner or (Student) of TM aid their ability in maintaining the mantra by enhancing the experience through using some form of substance (like marijuana) or a psychedelic (Hallucinogenic) drug to increase clarity of the mental conditioning with an upheaval (feeling Euphoric) and bring the emotional aspect so "psyched-out" that it becomes labeled as a "spiritual awakening".

The individual can no longer equate reality from fictional conjuring and may view it with the illusion of supernatural proportions.

This is a classic example of a false spiritual awakening, since it is nothing more than man attempting to find his Inner-Self through self-induced psychotic posturing and illusion. In time repeated practice becomes a form of brainwashing.

The argument is that man does not have a spiritual experience with himself, and that self-reliance does not strengthen an individual's inner-self, but in fact weakens their ability to reason beyond the knowledge or experience they have endured through their own life's sojourn.

*   *   *   *   *   *

One of the largest existential philosophies turned religion is Buddhism. It is the master of all Eastern Mystical Transcendence.

The transcending belief is that: Every living being has the same basic wish – to be happy and to avoid suffering. Even newborn babies, animals, and insects have this wish. It has been the main wish since beginningless time and it is present all the time, even during our sleep. Everyone spends their whole life working hard to fulfill this wish.

The expansive fortitude behind this philosophy is: Problems arise only if we respond to difficulties with a negative state of mind. Therefore, if we want to be free from problems, we must learn to control our mind.

Born out of India (circa 563BCE) in what is now modern-day Nepal, Siddhārtha Gautama, also known as Gautama Buddha (Shayamuni) was proclaimed as Buddha, meaning "Awakened One" or Enlightened One" sometime during his mid-adulthood.

No written records about Gautama have been found from his lifetime.

The sources for the life of Siddhārtha Gautama are a variety of different and sometimes conflicting traditional biographies.

Of these is the Buddhacarita, the earliest full biography of the man, which is an epic poem written by the poet Aśvaghoṣa, and dating around the beginning of the 2nd century CE.

Nevertheless, in most Buddhist traditions, Siddhārtha Gautama is regarded as the Supreme Buddha (Pali *sammāsambuddha*, Sanskrit *samyaksaṃbuddha*) of our age.

The traditional folklore that expounds him as the Buddha is that Gautama is said to have developed supra-mundane abilities including: a painless birth conceived without intercourse; no need for sleep, food, medicine, or bathing. He was claimed to be omniscience and have the ability to "suppress karma".

As well, he is also believed to have possessed what Buddhist believe are "the 32 Signs of the Great Man". The big one among these is having Blue Eyes, perfect Skin Tone and a Beautiful Appearance.

Nevertheless, some of the more ordinary details of his life have been gathered from non-traditional sources.

In modern times there has been an attempt to form a secular understanding of Siddhārtha Gautama's life by omitting the traditional supernatural elements of his early biographies.

The traditional aspects of the Buddhist religion are the four (4) Steps of Enlightenment and different levels of reincarnation that an individual needs to go through in order achieve full enlightenment and reach Nirvāṇa.

The four (4) Steps of Enlightenment are: Insight, Knowledge, Freedom and Nirvāṇa.

Another is to worship the Teacher who is working through Karma towards the levels of Enlightenment and renounce the student who is below any subsequent levels of transcendence and on a confused but noble path towards enlightenment and the final reincarnated state of Nirvāṇa (Pāli: Nibbāna) and attain the spiritual awakening called *bodhi;* and understand reality.

Siddhārtha Gautama lived to be 80 years of age, but before the Buddha announced that he would soon reach Parinirvana (the eternal true self), or the final deathless state and abandon his earthly body, he was to eat his final meal, which is said to have been pig meat or pig like.

Sometime after eating the meal, he became very sick. Some believe he suffered food poisoning, but before he left his earthly body, he told a person close to him that it wasn't the food that was causing his death.

He most definitely did not want to be seen as dying by nature or unnatural human means but wanted to fulfill the Chandra of his pronounced deity; much as what the Pharaoh of Egypt did in proclaiming himself as "RA", the sun god or God on earth.

It was supposed that when the Pharaoh left his earthly body, he did so by means of his own ability and free will in order to show his deity.

Even though Buddha was born out of India and revered in that region, the disciplines of Buddha sojourned into China and throughout all of the Orient (now regarded as Asia) and the philosophy quickly set an accord with that part of the world.

Some early Chinese Taoist-Buddhists thought Buddha to be a reincarnation of Lao Tzu, known as Laozi (also Lao-Tsu, or Lao-Tze) a philosopher and poet of ancient China around the 4th century BC.

These two images, in time, became morphed into the one icon and familiar character of a short, fat, "Big Bellied" smiling Buddha you see in most Chinese Restaurants and statuette stores.

This has traditionally represented an icon of "good luck" or "wealth" in different Asian cultures and tries to project a religion of peace and happiness, especially if they are gold plated images.

In India the image of Buddha looks like a Hindu and in China and throughout Asia the image looks Asian.

In modern times Buddhism is more prevalent towards the Asian culture and not India, mainly because the Hindu's worship over 300 million gods and Buddha is not the chief god in that region, Brahman is.

Buddha was born, lived for 80 years, died (circa 483 BCE) and was cremated.

What remains of his legacy are reincarnations and incantations of many different Buddha's, which through the centuries have perpetuated the myth and legend of Siddhārtha Gautama's claim as the Pali- sammāsambuddha, and a philosophy which has transcended both myth and legend.

* * * * * *

The battle within us all is that **we are spirit beings having a human experience** and this causes us to constantly search for something above and beyond ourselves.

All of us have moments where we feel empty and aloof, as if there is a part of us missing and is "out there" somewhere and we need to interconnect with it.

There's not one of us who hasn't looked up at the evening sky and wondered how all of that came about and do we have some connection with the cosmos, either physical or spiritual.

Likewise, we also contemplate if there is other life like ours out there in the vastness of a seemingly endless universe with billions of galaxies and countless potential "Life Supporting" planets.

As a race of creatures that have control over the entire earth and everything within it, we are constantly searching for the true meaning of life and our reason for existence or "Being".

Mankind has been looking to find that missing piece to the puzzle since the beginning of our existence.

We create folklore concepts which try to reason through our physical constraints of science and deductive reasoning that "Missing Link", where all life had its beginning, but to no avail.

It seems that we have not evolved far enough yet to either intellectually understand or transcend Enlightenment of the Cosmic Order, so the discovery appears before us, as if a veil has been lifted from our eyes and we see with clear and precise vision.

Our intellect is beyond any other creature that roams this planet, but intellect cannot in and of itself substantiate the single most sought-after questions: "Why is it we are here" and "is this all there is, to be born and then to die and be no more?"

There appears to be a common aspect to all existence in the universe, starting right here on planet Earth and extending into the farthest outreach of what appears to be the outer edge of our universe (14 billion light-years away) where planets, galaxies, stars, and all forms of existence continues in a re-cycling of birth to death and then rebirth. It seems perpetual but isn't.

The universe has a known point of beginning and speculative point of ending.

By the laws of physics and motion, through kinetic extensionality the physical universe will eventually, in a given portion and passage of time, consume itself up.

The process and property of gravity, which was the leading factor in creating the celestial universe as we see and know it, will be the same process and property that exhausts all matter and energy into non-existence.

The Good News is that if the Bible is the true and concise Word of the Creator of the Universe, then 1) mankind does not just evolve into a state of non-existence, and 2) the universe does not just evolve into a state of non-existence; but rather all things are given a rebirth into a new "State of Being" and everlasting transference which like God, has no Beginning and no End (Reference the Book of Revelation Chapters 21 and 22).

*   *   *   *   *   *

Now let's look into what is considered some "Far-Out" or "Out of this World" Agnostic Theorizing.

Most of these theorists are humanistic with no religious or theological convictions and a small group who consider themselves to be atheists; but there are also some Christians who have been sucked into this as a cult following due to supernatural or Sci-Fi infatuations.

There has been some speculation, conjured up by conspiracy theorists with no real factual evidence, that we (Humans) are the droppings of a cosmic alien race, who as wandering celestial sojourns thousands of years ago came across the Earth and saw it as an inhabitable planet and began an assimilation as the superior life form with the already primitive and primal life which were indigenous to this planet.

As well, within the same group of conspirators there are others who claim physical and symbolic evidence that thousands of years ago (maybe even hundreds of thousands of years), cosmic alien race(s) had visited the Earth and helped establish many civilizations all over the planet while human life (Man) was in its Pre-historic state and that these alien race(s) inter-breed (had sex) with humans and helped primitive man evolve into the super race of homo-sapiens that have ruled this planet for the last ten thousand to one hundred thousand years.

The evidence that was left behind by these so-called "extra-terrestrials" are gigantic monoliths and super structures and what look like airfields (Landing Zones) which required technology far beyond the capabilities of the humans that lived during the time they were developed.

World-wide archeological findings of advanced symbols of language, artifacts and scientific inventiveness do not match the fossil remains of the human life living during the time period being excavated.

None of these are explainable and neither archeologists, zoologists, biologists, genealogists, sociologists nor any other kind of "ologist" has the answer, just a lot of speculation and non-scientific conspirator mumbo-jumbo.

I guess for some, it's easier to believe in something that is on the other side of the God spectrum but still has to be supernatural.

ET fills that void with "Super Beings" that could possibly be a savior for mankind, distantly "Out There" with superhuman qualities and extreme advanced technologies, but yet somehow connected to us through cosmic parenting.

Something that could be a wonderful counselor and friend to the human race who understands our sinful nature and imperfections, rather than an over-lording God figure who is going to chastise us and cast us into eternal damnation because of these traits.

It's interesting that every time a scientist starts to explain the origins of human sociological evolution or super technological intercessions, they always have to refer to the beginning of that origin as coming from something that is superior to the human race, outside the confines of our slow and primitive scientific processes, which in our past took centuries to develop even a single theorem; just as the alien conspirators are looking towards the heavens for the answer of our origin as coming from something superior to us.

It kind of makes sense from the atheistic and agnostic type of consciousness and mindset, that we, with all of our imperfections could not have developed and implemented advanced technological feats while still in a primordial state of existence thousands of years ago, or for that matter just a few hundreds of years ago; considering the great minds of our modern scientific institutions have concluded that we had to evolve into our present state of advanced technology and knowledge.

The Bible does however speak of a Super Race of humans referred to as the Nephilim. These were Fallen Angels (demonic spirits) who manifested themselves in human form and were referred to as "the sons of God", who in their demonic form came upon the daughters of men and they bore children to them.

Those were the Giants and mighty men of old and renowned stature (Genesis 6:4).

The Nephilim came upon the earth after the fall of man (Adam) and before the Flood of Noah, when men's hearts and actions had become set on every form of evil and abomination towards God, which was identified as being enticed by these creatures and the primary reason God brought the Flood upon the earth to kill all of mankind (except 8 people-Noah and his family) and remove the sin which had filled the entire earth (Genesis 6:5-8).

This occurred again sometime later after the flood when Noah's lineage had reestablished the earth and these demonic spirits once again came upon the daughters of men and created Nephilim, later referred to as Anakim, but to a much lesser extent than before the Flood.

Israel during the time of Moses while preparing to enter into the Promised Land that God had given Abraham, fought against an Amorite King named Og, who ruled in the northern region of Bashan which occupied part of the Promised Land.

This King was said to be one of the descendants of the Nephilim and when Israel overtook the region and killed the King, he was measured to be four cubits wide (6 feet) and over nine cubits tall (14 feet).

The peoples who inhabited the Land God was preparing for Israel were the Canaanites, Amorites, Hittites, Perizzites, Jebusites and Hivites.

All of these peoples possessed Nephilim (Anakim) within their tribes of people, and they posed a great threat to Israel and were an abomination in the sight of God.

God had commanded Israel to destroy all the Nephilim (Anakim) and eliminate the demonic seed of this race of giants from the hill country in Hebron, Debir, Anab and in all the hill country of Israel and Judah, which God did through Joshua and the army of Israel (Joshua 11:21-23).

The Philistines also had a race of these incestuous humans in their lineage.

King David of Israel fought against and defeated the chief warrior of the Philistine's named Goliath, the Philistine Giant and sacked their army (1Samuel 17:4-54).

God had decided to end the demonic incestuous activity of these demon spirits from mating with human women and producing any more of this lineage on the earth by placing them in isolation (Incarcerating them into the Abyss).

In the New Testament of the Holy Bible, the Letter from Jude in verse 6 tells us regarding what God has done; *"Remember the angels who did not stay within the limits of their proper authority but abandoned their own dwelling place (Heaven): they are bound with eternal chains in the darkness below where God is keeping them for that Great Day on which they will be condemned."*

Nevertheless, there has been skeleton remains and fossil excavations of these giants in clustered groupings and the conspiracy theorists claim this indicates a possible organized civilization of these people as aliens and either isolating themselves from the indigenous homo-sapiens of this planet or ruling over and becoming "Masters" of the Human Race, who were physically and intellectually inferior to these giants.

It is interesting that the fossil remains of these giants can be found throughout the Middle East and even Europe, with estimates of being as tall as fourteen to twenty-five feet in height but are all prehistoric on the human evolution timetable.

This would give credence to the Biblical account concerning these people as Nephilim and their demise.

If these creatures were actually Aliens from distant Outer Space or off-shoots of a human hybrid caused by Alien interbreeding, then the evolutionary process would still have some form of them in existence to this day (I'm not talking about seven-foot three-inch basketball players, those aren't giants, just really tall guys with an overactive Pituitary Gland.)

The fossil evidence shows that these giants and the human race as we know it today existed at the same time, yet our species still exists, but they have completely disappeared.

There are a lot of things which have been reported and are still being reported concerning alien encounters, alien abductions, UFO sightings, strange noises coming out of the earth or loud booms which shake the ground coming from somewhere high in the stratosphere and other such phenomena as the blowing of a trumpet or shofar, which are all unexplainable from our modern scientific perspective.

There is no concrete or reliable evidence to date of any Extraterrestrial Existence in the form of an ET (Human like) or distinctively human like extraterrestrial fossil remains having been on earth.

What we have are fuzzy and blurred photographs of lights in the sky and what looks like a spacecraft floating or zooming across the horizon or rubber like dummies with odd, shaped eyes and heads scaring people into believing they have encountered something extraterrestrial.

I had mentioned earlier in this chapter that **we are spirit beings having a human experience** and this causes us to constantly search for something above and beyond ourselves.

Because we are created by God and in His Image, it is inherent within our inner self (our spirit) to have awareness that there is something "out there" above us.

God has implanted that knowledge in us and reveals it to us within the environment He has placed us in (the Earth); it is all around us constantly in nature, in the sky visible both day and night and through the written testimony of God through the Holy Spirit and to man by means of the written Word of God (Holy Bible).

I've done a lot of research on this; a whole lot of "Hands-On" over the last forty (40) years.

I believe beyond doubt that these things which are being witnessed in the sky and encountered by humans on this earth are indeed extraterrestrial, but not by physical beings from a distant galaxy and planet, but a spiritual encounter of a demonic manifestation, which of course would appear to be aliens to us.

It is in the realm of the Supernatural and not the Cosmic Universe.

The author has two undergraduate degrees in physics/geology and sociology and as a person schooled in the Sciences, I had already formulated an idea and concept regarding inter-dimensional cross-over while I was in college, which I was calling "Time Corridor Phasing".

In another book I've had published, "*Why Do Good Things Happen To Bad People*", I put forth this concept as a supposition with what I found was supported by Biblical Truth and Spiritual Guidance and insight from ADONAI.

The theorem of my idea takes matter (Mass) outside of the 3rd dimensional spectrum into the next levels of dimensional phasing (existence) through spiritual portals (or what I term as Corridors), by the transference of energy from physical matter into pure energy with no mass (Spirit), which could be existing and occupying in the same space of the previous dimensional level, but not visible to it because it is Time Phased at a much faster dimensional partition (frequency) rate and therefore, the matter (Mass) does not physically occupy the same space in the lower dimensional levels, but still occupies the same partitioned quadrant of space in a Time Phase Corridor.

The speed of travel within these dimensional corridors cannot be expressed in physical science or mathematics because it exists beyond the capability to comply with the Laws of Physics or applied science within our physical existence in the 3rd dimensional level.

The same is true in reverse with pure energy (Spirit) coming from the higher levels of dimensional time phasing down to the lower levels.

At each level they can be physically seen and co-exist from Higher to Lower and in reverse.

It appears that the difference with Spirit Beings created at the Higher Dimensional Levels than with humans, is they have the authority and ability from God to transform from their created forms or existing levels of dimensional existence downward to the lower levels, materializing at the 3rd dimensional level (physical creation) where we exist and physically interact with us.

Jesus also mentioned in the Gospel of Matthew, chapter 26, verse 53, how He could, at any time request from the Father for assistance from Heaven and God would dispatch twelve legions of angels to Him immediately.

My supposition is greatly supported by physical evidence which I myself have testified to as a witness.

I have physically witnessed the manifestation of Angelic Beings numerous times within the last forty (40) years. I mention this in detail in "*Why Do Good Things Happen To Bad People*".

They appeared within seconds out of nothing into a form that looked human, but in dynamic appearance and personality; and in the same way disappeared in the twinkling of an eye or into transparence as if you could see through them as they faded away.

They were very large at least nine feet tall and were not spirits of darkness or in an image like the Nephilim, but rather from the Abode of God, who are in the Presence of Almighty God.

Their faces were like polished copper and hair like spun gold, they had chiseled body features (like body builders) in physical appearance and shown the Glory of God through them; you could tell that they had been standing in front of and always reflected the image of being a servant of God.

There was a great and overwhelming feeling of peaceful strength coming from them that filled the entire areas they manifested themselves at, with great power that you could tell was not coming from them, but rather emanating through them from somewhere else, from a much higher level.

It was as if they manifested a visible point of an open corridor which reflected the higher dimensional level of Radiance, Power and Essence (Glory) from the Abode of God. The best example I can give in comparison with the known science of physics in our Dimensional Corridor of Time and existence, is Fiber Optics.

Where you have a long Optical Fiber Cable (made from multiple layered special glass strands coated with acrylate polymer or polyimide) and an optical laser energy source at one end.

In quantum mechanics the laser produces an amplified light source of photons through a process called "spontaneous emission", to be concentrated around one wavelength of light (Hyper-Condensing) and travel in an unrestricted linear path through the cable to the other end where the radiated brilliance and energy remains constant through the cable corridor and exits at the other end with the exact amount of originated energy and brilliance, as if coming from the original source of energy.

In layman terms and understanding it could be referred to as reflecting the image of the original source through a manifested image of a different kind, but that would be totally incorrect.

It's not reflecting the image but rather sustaining the original composition and structure of the energy source as if being right in front of it.

The Fallen Angels that God cast out of His Presence and His Abode (Heaven) are bound to the lower levels of the Physical Universe, with exception of Satan who still has audience and the ability to stand before the Most High God as the Accuser of the brethren and Children of God, but that ability is short lived and will be taken away from him eventually.

They still have the power of transference between Dimensional Levels through Time Phasing and can manifest themselves in physical images (deceiving appearance or unnatural forms) to us at the 3rd dimensional level.

I believe the UFO phenomena we have been witnessing over the millenniums and more so in this dispensational age are not alien visitations from Outer Space, but in fact demonic spiritual manifestations and not Extraterrestrials from the Cosmos.

There is more factual evidence through the Bible of this being demonic than all of the alien speculative eye witnessing with no empirical or scientific evidence, just folklore or "trust me" hear-say, and these people are constantly searching with no findings of physical evidence. You would think that throughout all the centuries of sightings and supposed landings, these Extraterrestrials would have left behind something of their technologies as evidence of their visits. I mean, look at all the hardware we left behind from our visits to the moon, we literally left tons of our existence there.

*   *   *   *   *   *

The occult has been growing world-wide at a rate that will exceed what it was during the Middle-Ages (Dark Ages) before this decade ends in 2030.

The occult is not humanism or atheism, it is spiritualism.

It is defined as supernatural and mystical, the practice of magic and sorcery, the belief in the paranormal and spiritual upheaval (demonic depravity).

The occult base their practices around mystery and a hidden society.

They are outside the sphere of monotheism or polytheism, there is no deity, just substance and matter and the manipulation of the natural forces that make up the physical universe and the spirits that control those forces.

The attractiveness of the occult is the forbidden mystery and enchanting mysticism of incantations and geometric symbols that exhibit supernatural powers.

It gives the illusion that the one who is performing the acts has the power to do such things, but the reality is that the manipulation is being performed by demonic spirits that have been summoned and are performing sinister acts through and for their human hosts.

Because these are lying spirits of darkness and delusion their purpose is to deceive and withhold the truth from their human counterparts and keep them in darkness, away from the Light of Truth, which is found through Faith in Jesus the Christ.

Their sorcery and magic is an abomination to God and eventually will devour everyone and everything that involves the practice of their evil.

God tells us explicitly through His Word to not indulge in the practices of the occult.

[Leviticus 19:26b - *"Do not practice any kind of magic."*]

[Leviticus 20:6-7 - *If any of you go for advice from anyone who consults the spirits of the dead, I will turn against you and will no longer consider you one of my people. Keep yourselves holy, because I Am the Lord your God."*]

[Deuteronomy 18:10-13 - *"Do not sacrifice your children in the fires on your altars; and don't let your people practice divination or look for omens or use spells or charms, and don't let them consult the spirits of the dead. The Lord your God hates people who do these disgusting things...be completely faithful to the Lord."*]

[Malachi 3:5a - *But people will tell you, ask for messages from fortunetellers and mediums, who chirp and mutter. They will say, after all, people should ask for messages from the spirits and consult the dead-on behalf of the living. You are to answer them, "Listen to what the Lord is teaching you! Don't listen to mediums-what they tell you cannot keep trouble away."*]

[Isaiah 8:19-20 - *The Lord Almighty says, "I will appear among you to judge, and I will testify at once against those who practice magic..."*]

[Revelation 20:14-15 - *Then death and the world of the dead were thrown into the Lake of Fire (this Lake of Fire is the second death). Those who did not have their names written in the Book of the Living were thrown into the Lake of Fire.*]

[Revelation 21:8 - "*But cowards, traitors, perverts, murderers, the immoral, those who practice magic, those who worship idols, and all liars-the place for them is the lake burning with fire and sulfur, which is the second death.*"]

The biggest deception for most Believers in Christ is to think that some of these occult practices are acceptable if done within or under the guise of a church ministry.

As if because a Pastor or Youth Pastor or a member of a Christian Fellowship performs a magic act, then it is not an unclean act, it's just good old-fashioned fun...nothing could be farther from the Truth!

The impression is that the Christian will clean it up and make sure that no real deception is performed in the presence of God's people and God most likely "looks the other way" and not see it as defiled, as He does with the horrible heathen magicians.

I've even seen magic acts performed in the presence of a Sunday Church Fellowship Service as part of a special entertainment act and the fellow doing the magic act was calling himself "The Christian Magician", what an oxymoron.

It was a side business he did in his "past Life" before he came to Christ, for a little extra money. He even had business cards and would perform at birthday parties or any fellowship event a church may be holding.

Yeshua never pulled a rabbit out of a hat or did any illusions that would make anyone believe that He was performing an act that wasn't real or not guided by the hand of God the Father.

The Enemy of God knows exactly how to deceive mankind (especially Christians) into believing a lie, especially in the current dispensational age, the Church of Laodicea, which is the Lukewarm Church.

Human self-righteousness and ego are the best tools for the powers of darkness to invade a Christian's Faith and invoke temptation on individuals to bring about doubt, which leads to unfaithfulness and questions what the Word of God has pronounced.

The appearance of innocence with something that is declared evil is the illusion that the powers of darkness give to justify that something unholy is holy, that's why they are all called Liars; and the Evil One was called by Jesus, "*a liar and the father of lies*". (John 8:44)

*   *   *   *   *   *

Polytheism or Pagan worship has similarities to the occult in that they practice rituals which incorporate summoning spirits of the dead and divination.

There is such a thing as pagan religion, where a spiritual based theology has established into a religious doctrine and dogma around an ordinance which is non-biblical and non-monotheist.

Polytheism is the worship of many different gods under the same cultural setting.

It has dominated most of human history from a religious type of view.

The best-known example of polytheism in ancient times is Greek/Roman mythology (Zeus, Apollo, Aphrodite, Poseidon, etc.).

The clearest modern example of polytheism is Hinduism, which has over 300 million gods.

Although Hinduism is, in essence, pantheistic (which is philosophical in the belief that the universe or nature as the totality of everything, is identical with divinity, or that everything composes an all-encompassing, immanent God), it does hold to religious beliefs and worshipping in many gods.

The main emphasis of the teachings within Hinduism are through the Bhagavad Gītā, spoken by Krishna, the Upanishads (which are knowledge) and the essence of the Vedas (which are eternal truth).

While the Vedas focus on rituals, the Upanishads focus on spiritual insight and philosophical teachings and discuss the chief god Brahman and reincarnation.

It is interesting to note that even in polytheistic religions; one god usually reigns supreme over the other gods (e.g., Zeus in Greek/Roman mythology and Brahman in Hinduism).

The Bible clearly teaches against polytheism.

[Exodus 20:3-5a - *"worship no god but me. Do not make for yourselves images of anything in heaven or on earth or in the water under the earth. Do not bow down to any idol or worship it, because I Am the Lord your God and I tolerate no rivals."*]

[Deuteronomy 6:4 - *"Hear, O Israel: The LORD our God, the LORD is one."*]

[Psalm 96:5 - *"For all the gods of the nations are idols, but the LORD made the heavens."*]

[James 2:19 - *"Do you believe that there is one God. Good! Even the demons believe and tremble with fear."*]

In speaking to the High Council of Greek Scholars on Mars Hill in Athens, the Apostle Paul stood in the midst of the Areopagus and said, "*Men of Athens, I observe that you are very religious in all respects. For while I was passing through and examining the objects of your worship, I also found an altar with this inscription, 'TO AN UNKNOWN GOD.' Therefore what you worship in ignorance, this I proclaim to you, (there is only one God; there are false gods and those who pretend to be gods, but there is only one God), He does not dwell in temples made with hands; nor is He served by human hands, as though He needed anything, since He Himself gives to all people life and breath and all things*" (Acts 17:22-25)

The first two humans created were from their very beginning in the presence of God and actually walking with God in an area that He had set aside on the Earth with perfection and beauty, resembling what could be manifested in physical form from what was Spiritual perfection in Heaven, the closes thing to a paradise on Earth, the Garden of Eden. They had face-to-face fellowship with the Spirit of the One True God (YAHWEH).

Before the fall of man, Adam had no idea of the knowledge of good and evil and only knew what was put before him in purity of wisdom and knowledge; he was devoid of sin and could receive all things from God in full strength without apprehension or doubt; he was innocent. Even though sin was an inherent part of his flesh, having been made from the ground of the earth, sin had not yet been activated through his flesh.

In our fallen state, the human form of understanding what is spiritual does not go beyond our five anatomic senses or what we can explain through deductive arbitration of physical evidence.

It must bring about a final conclusion which is substantiated through physical evidence which is backed by the laws of nature (physics and science) and social order and governing laws.

Reasoning is based on factual evidence that you can study and observe.

It does not give claim to what is invisible or under the suspicion of thoughts, dreams or cosmic conspiracy.

From ancient times up until this current age of advanced science and instant access to information and knowledge, paganism essentially exists in the same format.

The ancient pagans believed that the physical sun was the source of all life and believed it to be the god of all life.

In these modern times, pagans still believe the same thing and react in the same manner.

The Pharaoh of ancient Egypt was considered to be God on earth and worshiped as the sun god "RA".

The ancient pagans believed the earth was the mother god (Terra Mater or Gaia) and sustained life.

In these modern times pagans still believe the same thing and call the earth "Mother Earth" and ecologists worship the earth as such.

The ancient pagans-built temples and monoliths which reflected their belief in the physical celestial mysteries of the star gods and invented characters as constellations from the heavenly bodies and named them according to the gods they represented.

Modern pagans still worship these gods at the formation of monoliths to perform the ancient pagan rites and rituals.

Soothsayers and fortunetellers use astrology as a means to predict present and future human events.

One of the world renowned ancient pagan worship sites which is still being used in these modern times is located on the Salisbury Plain of Wiltshire, England known as "Stonehenge", which means Upright Rock Enclosure.

Another comes from the ancient Maya Civilization which spread throughout the Mesoamerica geography (now called Central America) in the form of monolithic pyramid structures called the Mayan Temple in Belize.

Throughout the world there are many different pagan structures and monoliths that reflect the religious archeology which was part of their civilization's infrastructure and social government system.

All had a direct influence on the behavior and actions to which they believed in satisfying their gods edicts and the place they would have in the "Here-After" by doing so.

Some of these actions are viewed from our modern-day perspective as no less than barbaric or demonic in nature.

There are two aspects of paganism that deserve some attention and scrutiny.

First is an interesting comparison that both paganism and monotheism have in common - "Blood Sacrifice".

That a blood sacrifice must be made in order for appeasing and atonement to be made to the gods or to God.

The monotheistic view of Atonement through Judaism was by blood sacrifice made through symbolic appeasement of certain animals.

According to the Law of Moses, God gave the Children of Israel rites of Atonement through the Levitical Priesthood and Sin Offerings by the blood sacrifice of appointed animals which represented certain human sin natures and characteristics.

[Leviticus 17:11 - *"For the life of a creature is in the blood, and I have given it to you to make atonement for yourselves on the altar; it is the blood that makes atonement for one's life."*]

This is why Abel's offering to the Lord God was acceptable and Cain's was not. Abel gave an animal offering to God as a blood sacrifice, while Cain's was seen unacceptable and lazy for offering a grain offering from the earth.

The purpose of the Sin Offerings was to give a temporal appeasement so that the Wrath of God would not consume them, and the Levitical Atonement Offering of the Lamb pointed to the final Offering of appeasement that God would accept for the completion of the Eternal Forgiveness of Sin through the death and resurrection of the Son of God (Yeshua ADONAI - the Man God or Messiah) as the Lamb of God.

Thus, God Himself was standing in place of the temporal sacrifice according to the Law in order to give sanctification from withholding Judgment against the Law.

This now allows all mankind to share in the Eternal Sanctification of the Sin Offering made through the Grace of God and the Mercy He gave on the Cross when Jesus became that Eternal Sacrifice once and forever.

Now, if we acknowledge our sinful nature through a point of heartfelt repentance, that we have sinned against God and need His forgiveness and turn towards His Forgiveness through Faith in the Son of God (Yeshua ADONAI), then we will receive the Atonement of our sins and propitiation forever and become Children of God, then share in the Presence of His Eternal Glory forever.

The pagan view of atonement has sinister overtones and does not recognize the sinful nature of man nor atoning for sin but rather showing reverence and submission to deities and demigods or cultural entities.

They too give blood sacrifice, but in order to summon evil spirits or demonic entities to aid them in some way or to ward off and appease these demonic forces so that they will not harm them or give them luck and good fortune.

In most cases where there is a festival honoring the chief god, the sacrifice demanded is a human.

Many times, you'll see idols of these false gods in their places of worship or sacrifice and hanging around the necks of the tribal priests in order to show the presence of the deity power and authority.

In these times this fashion is still in place in pagan temples around the world and even as displayed by those that worship such gods by displaying them in their homes or automobiles hanging from the driving mirrors or placed on top of dashboards.

In ancient times many cultures where paganism was practiced, sacrificed their children at the burning altar of a god or a young virgin as a show of purity.

A few practiced cannibalisms and mixed that into the form of their religion.

The use of hallucinogenic herbal substances or smoking peyote while performing tribal dancing and even engaging in group orgies, builds up a hyper-psychotic trance state which after hours of incantations leads to mass hysteria in performing the sacrificial act; it can be brutal and demonic. Some of these practices and ritual rites are still in place during these modern times.

A perfect example of a pagan god and demonic worship form from the biblical perspective, was the worship of Ba'al.

Ba'al was the largest pagan worship in the Old Testament times during Israel's forty years of wandering in the desert and became a plague on Israel.

The Lord God had told Israel through the Law of Moses to not worship any other gods but Him. It was the first of the Ten Commandments He had given through Moses.

In the TANAKH under the Book of Numbers chapter 25 verses 1-5 it speaks of God's Wrath towards His people for doing such a thing.

[*While the Israelites were camped at Acacia, some of the men had sex with Moabite women. These women then invited the men to ceremonies where sacrifices were offered to their gods. The men ate the meat from the sacrifices and worshiped the Moabite gods.*

The LORD was angry with Israel because they had worshiped the god Ba'al Peor. So, he said to Moses, "Take the Israelite leaders who are responsible for this and have them killed in front of my sacred tent where everyone can see. Maybe then I will stop being angry with the Israelites."

Moses told Israel's officials, "Each of you must put to death any of your men who worshiped Ba'al."]

The final show of God's disapproval and end of the Ba'al worship in Israel was through the Prophet Elijah.

The Lord God finally had Elijah confront the prophets of Ba'al (450 of them) out of Samaria to a challenge at Mount Carmel between the Lord God of Israel and the god Ba'al to show all of Israel the Lord their God was the one and only God.

This show of power was not to enhance God's power over Ba'al, but to show that the pagan god was of no consequence at all; it was a false deity and had no power or authority to begin with.

The challenge was to build an altar and give a pronounced sacrifice to both the god Ba'al and an Altar and pronounced sacrifice to the Most High God of Israel and see which one would come down and receive their sacrifice by consuming it by fire from heaven. (1Kings chapter 18)

As the prophets of Ba'al called upon their god to receive and consume their sacrifice, no answer was ever given to their requests, no power from Ba'al was shown, just silence.

As they keep pleading and begging for Ba'al to come down and receive their sacrifice, Elijah began denouncing their actions and scoffing them as foolish men who worshiped a false god.

As their pleas fell on the deaf ears of their false god, they began cutting themselves with sharp knives and daggers until their blood flowed down them, but to no avail.

After many hours, Elijah finally gathered them altogether and in the presence of Israel called upon the Most High God to receive his sacrifice.

Suddenly the Lord sent fire down from Heaven and completely consumed and burned up the sacrifice and even the ground around the entire area of the Altar.

Great fear came up all that witnessed the mighty act of God, as they knew that what they had witnessed was from the Lord and proclaimed, "*The Lord alone is God!*"

The Lord God had given them over to Elijah; he then ordered that all of the prophets of Ba'al be taken down to the Kishon Brook and they were all killed. (1Kings 18:39-40)

Once again, the Lord God told Israel that He and He alone was God and that He would share with no rivals.

*   *   *   *   *   *

Secularism is anything that is humanistic or macro-political and absolutely non-monotheistic.

Even though not practiced as a religion (from the spiritual sense), secularism is the belief in the human race as being supreme and everyone is God-like to some degree (the creator and actor of their own destiny).

Worship is the feeling or expression of reverence and adoration for a deity.

In many instances worship can be mistaken for admiration of something that is not a deity or religious sanctification.

There is worship of secular things which become idols of psychological and physical dependency and compulsions, such as obsessions with: celebrities, food, sex, drugs, education (obtaining more and more human knowledge) careers, money, marriage, children, nature (the Earth Environmentalists), pets, hobbies...you name it and it can become a point of obsession and secular worship.

There is such a thing as secular religion, where a Christian based theology has established their religious doctrine and dogma around a constitution or ordinance which is non-biblical.

The belief that everyone is a Child of God no matter if they accept Jesus the Christ as their Lord and Savior or follow the ordinances of the Holy Bible.

This of course undermines the ordinances of the Word of God and is a lie and the ones preaching it are liars. [*1John 2:22 - Who, then, is the liar? It is those who say that Jesus is not the Messiah. Such people are the Enemy of Christ - they reject both the Father and the Son.*]

There is no one big family of humanity under God known as His Children.

Out of Forgiveness comes our Salvation

We (human beings) are all His creation, created in His Image as the highest order of His Creation and have sinned against His Holiness and all deserve death as the payment of our sins, yet we have all been given the opportunity and ability to receive His Salvation under Faith in Yeshua ADONAI (Jesus the Christ).

That if we believe He is the Son of God (Messiah) and died for the forgiveness of all the sins we could ever commit; and call upon His Holy Name in complete and total heartfelt repentance and receive Him into our Hearts as our personal Lord and Savior, then we shall be saved and become the sons and daughters (children) of the Most High God (Yeshua ADONAI).

This is the Truth, and this is Eternal Life! (John 1:1-3, John 1:14, John 8:42, John 14:6-12, Matthew 16:15-16, Romans 3:24-26, Romans 10:9-10, 1Corinthians 15:28, Colossians 1:15-16, Titus 2:13, 2Peter 1:1, 1John 5:19-20, Revelation 22:12-13, Revelation 22:16)

*   *   *   *   *   *

A perfect example of a secular religion is the modern Episcopal Church, where the ordination of women and homosexuals are being consecrated as part of their Pastor Clergy and is now an acceptable practice within their religious order.

This is taboo under the Biblical Commands from God in the Old and New Testaments.

Homosexuality is strongly denounced by God many times throughout the Holy Bible as an abomination and physical perversion.

[Leviticus 18:22 – *No man is to have sexual relations with another man; God hates that.*]

[Leviticus 20:13 – *If a man has sexual relations with another man, they have done a disgusting thing, and both shall be put to death. They are responsible for their own death.*]

[Romans 1:26-27 – *Because they do this (being perverted), God has given them over to shameful passions. Even the women pervert the natural use of their sex by unnatural acts. In the same way the men give up natural sexual relations with women and burn with passion for each other. Men do shameful things with each other, and as a result they bring upon themselves the punishment they deserve for their wrongdoing.*]

[1Corinthians 6:18-20 – *Avoid immorality. Any other sin a man (synonymous of male & female) commits does not affect his body; but the man who is guilty of sexual immorality sins against his own body. Don't you know that your body is the temple of the Holy Spirit who lives in you and who was given to you by God? You do not belong to yourselves but to God; He bought you for a price. So, use your bodies for God's Glory.*]

[Revelation 21:8 – "*But cowards, traitors, perverts, murderers, the immoral, those who practice magic, those who worship idols, and all liars-the place for them is the Lake burning with Fire and Sulfur (the Lake of Fire), which is the second death.*"]

As for women being ordained as Pastors or taking a leadership role within the Assembly of the Church; the Apostle Paul made it quite clear the Order of the Church and its Assembly.

Paul was given by Yeshua Himself the order and appointment to be the Apostle of the Gentiles and to establish the Church within the heathen nations throughout the world (Acts 9:1-19).

Paul made it quite clear the Order of the Church and its Assembly.

He pronounced under the guidance of the Holy Spirit, the actions and standard by which the leadership of the Church shall be given and maintained throughout the Church Age.

[Church Age - The time from which Jesus ascended from the Mount of Olives into Heaven and the physical return of the Lord back to the earth] (Acts 1:9-11).

Paul declared that there is no role of leadership for women in the Church under any circumstance or condition throughout the Church Age.

[1Corinthians14:33b-35 – *"because God does not want us to be in disorder but in harmony and peace. As in all the churches of God's people, the women should keep quite in the meetings. They are not allowed to speak; as the Jewish Law says, they must not be in charge. If they want to find out about something, they should ask their husbands at home. It is a disgraceful thing for a woman to speak in a church meeting."*]

[1Timothy 2:11-14 – *"Women should learn in silence and all humility. I do not allow them to teach or to have authority over men; they must be quiet. For Adam was created first and then Eve. And it was not Adam who was deceived; it was the woman who was deceived and broke God's law."*]

I don't believe that there is any misconception of the Gospel dictates regarding these issues, but only individuals who act in disobedience due to pride and a desire to willfully disregard the Commands of God. Pastors who are having marital issues and who want to appease their wives or just disregarding the order that was established from the beginning of the statutes which Paul had pronounced. There is no excuse for these actions except becoming secular to entitle personal desires and spur disobedience without regard for its outcome.

The Church is not ours, but the collective assembly of individuals who have been saved under the Blood Covenant of Jesus the Christ and whose names have been written in the Lambs Book of the Living.

The Evil One and powers of darkness are constantly working against the Church to find ways to deceive Believers in Christ (especially the Leadership of the Church) to give into modern secular thinking and political correctness.

To think and reason in human terms and not out of Godliness from the Mind of God (The Holy Spirit).

The fight for women's rights or equality for women is a social political and secular agenda and one that should not be an argument within the Assembly of the Church but is strictly a Humanistic view.

Equality is found only through Christ Jesus and our obedience to God through Him.

Whether Jesus was friendly to women and had them as followers within His group of disciples does not mean He was giving them the same status or authority He had given to the Men.

There is no reason for anyone believing in Yeshua to be fighting for their rights to anything, for ADONAI has promised to give us anything that we ask of Him through a request of faith in Yeshua' Name, but it requires heartfelt faith with no doubt in the request being presented to God (John 14:12-13). This is not limited to just Holy Men or the interpretation of any request to be justified as a righteous request according to what a Pastor or any other person in the church thinks about it, it's your request to your God uninhibited.

The written Word of God reflects the nature of God and how He wants us to interact with Him and among ourselves.

The theme behind what God projects is Faith, Hope and Love, and the greatest of these Virtues is Love.

The main Essence of God's nature is Love, *"Whoever does not love does not know God, because God is Love."* (1John 4:8)

What the secular church does is cause division and divide itself into segregated thinking and religious dogma and doctrine.

The fact that we have in Christianity so many different religious orders (Churches and Assemblies) and business affiliates only shows division and indulges the Church into the secular world order and causes great division.

In that kind of environment faith and agreement in what Christ stands for and what the truth is behind the scriptures is open to misinterpretation and false teaching.

It has ushered in the Church of Laodicea (the Lukewarm Church), which was told through the Revelation of Jesus the Christ to the Apostle John (Revelation 3:14-21).

This would be the last of the Seven Churches to represent the span of the Age of Grace, which is the time period the Church would exist on the earth until the Rapture, when Christ would take the "Church" (collective) out of the Earth. [1Thessalonians 4:16b-17 - *...and the dead in Christ will rise first. After that, we who are still alive and are left will be caught up together with them in the clouds to meet the Lord in the air. And so, we will be with the Lord forever.*]

The English interpretation of the Bible and the meaning behind what the transliteration is from Greek and Hebrew and then translated into Latin has been a scholastic endeavor since 1611 when the appointment of the King James Council attempted to bring it all together into one understandable literary reading through the common Middle English translation.

It is without doubt the Standard and Accepted English Translation in Christianity.

The finding of the Dead Sea scrolls and comparison between the original Hebrew Text and the transliteration from Hebrew in the King James English translation confirms it is linguistically and dialog correct, but not in textual content. There are some missing books of scrolls that have been deliberately left out or remove for the final assembly of text when the Bible was being assembled because of disagreement over the textual reliability. It also did not fit into the Cannon subscription and dogma that the scholastic interpreters would allow or agree upon. Such scrolls as the Book of Maccabees and the Book of Enoch, which appear in the Jewish Bible are not found in the English Bible. Other such writings of the Apostles Thomas, Bartholomew and Judas Thaddaeus were also omitted from the Gospel accounts because they did not fall in line with the accepted narrative requirements. This is also why there are areas within the content that vary in textual uniformity and led to counter interpretations and confusion.

Nevertheless, now the Bible and Scriptures had a common format for projecting what the Church wanted in understanding its content, so the layman could use without having to rely solely on a religious scholar or church leader to interpret (Pastor, Minister, Bishop, Priest...and the list goes on).

It is God who reveals the Truth through the Holy Spirit to the Church and to each and every individual within the Body of Christ who wishes to receive it. [1John 2:27 - *"But you have received the Holy Spirit, and he lives within you, so you don't need anyone to teach you what is true. For the Spirit teaches you everything you need to know, and what he teaches is true--it is not a lie. So just as he has taught you, remain in fellowship with Christ."*]

It is God and God alone who reveals the Truth!

CHAPTER III
(God is Truth)

The purest essence of Truth (*HaEmet*) can only be expressed through the Source of Its Creator, Who Is, Who Was and Who Is to come again (*Kadosh*), which is the Eternal Holiness of God (*Elohim*).

God is Spirit (*Ruach ADONAI*) and Eternal (*Ruach Olam*) and Holy (*Ruach HaKodesh*).

His Being is Pure Light, and all Righteousness and Truth comes from His Presence (*Gevurat Elohim*) and His Glory (*Shekinah*).

He Commands through His Word (*HaDavar*) all things into existence and sustains the existence of all Creation (in Heaven and on Earth) through the Word of Truth (*HaDavar Elohim*) in Faith without doubt.

In God the Truth is Eternal and Everlasting.

Through God it is Pure Substance of Light and Eternal Glory.

And God said, "*Let Light Be*" and His Light filled the void of darkness that was the vastness of the physical universe.

And God said, "*Let the Firmament Be*" and He caused the physical universe (all matter and substance) to come into existence and divided it into "Heaven" Sky and "Dry Land" Earth.

The Earth becomes the sole point where God references all of the physical universe and does so exclusively with the Earth because it is His Footstool, where He purposed life to be placed within the confines of the physical universe and to establish the Laws of Creation.

All other references to the firmament above the Earth (Outer Space) are in manners which either guide man's existence from earth using the stars to reference or point to the wonderment of God's physical creation and the celestial events that take place in the heavens (comets, meteors, solar and lunar eclipses, northern lights, sunrise, and sunset, etc).

And God Commanded, "*Let us make Man in Our image, after Our likeness*" and God took from the ground of the Earth and formed the likeness of Himself in the image of a human man and breathed into his nostrils the Holy Spirit (*Ruach HaKodesh*) and man became a Living Being.

The Man had the Holy Spirit within him, which was the Life-giving source of his being, and he was at this moment in a perfect state of being, without any sin and capable of interfacing with God the Creator (Face to Face).

Thus, Man (Human Beings) became the Highest Order of Creation in Reverence to God, creating man in His own image and breathing His Holy Spirit into man, giving him a special and unique position and purpose apart from all the other creatures that God had brought into existence, both in Heaven (The Abode of the Almighty) and on the Earth (His Footstool).

And God commanded the Man, "*Be fruitful and multiply and subdue the Earth*", thus instilling sexual reproduction.

God has revealed Himself to Mankind in a three-fold manner as The Father (*ABBA-HaElohim*), as The Son (*Ben HaElohim*) and as The Great and Mighty Holy Spirit (*Ruach HaKodesh*).

Likewise, God created man in a three-fold manner as body (physical), soul (mind intellect and conscience) and as spirit (human free-will, but dead to sin at the moment of conception).

It was when Man disobeyed the Command of God and committed sin against the Word of God through the act of disobedience and blasphemy, that God retracted the Holy Spirit from the man and his spirit went from being fully alive and intercessory with God (Face to Face), to becoming dead and sinful, apart from intercessory with God (no more Face to Face).

This is where the Lord God became distant and nonvisual any longer to man.

He would speak to man through his soul (mind) from His Spirit and man would be guided by his faith in having to believe and react to that which he could no longer see.

[Hebrews 11:1 - *"Now faith is confidence in what we hope for and assurance about what we do not see"*]

[Hebrews 11:6 - *And without faith it is impossible to please God, because anyone who comes to him must believe that he exists and that he rewards those who earnestly seek him"*]

It is not enough to call God good or righteous, for He is Holy (*Kadosh*).

God is Eternal, without any beginning and without any end (*Ruach Olam*).

He was Always and will Forever Be (*Ehyeh asher Ehueh*); yet He created man in His Image.

It is very important to realize who God is and what His Name is.

It is by His Name sake that we are saved. It is when we call upon the Name of the Lord in Faith that He gives us our Everlasting Salvation and Eternal Life.

God has always been a mystery in revealing His Name as a single Entity.

He is of Himself Holy and Divine, and He never revealed Himself by any name until Moses asked.

When Moses asked God what His name was so he could tell the Israelites who has sent him", the Lord God answered him, "*I AM that*

IAM", tell them the one who is called IAM (Ehyeh) send me to you." (Exodus 3:14)

Even upon this, God did not reveal a name by which to call Him.

It was an identity of the Highest Magnitude *(Ehyeh)* to describe His personage as Spirit, to a level that man could comprehend the existence of.

This would be conveyed through four Hebrew Consonants (Letters) as YHWH and be pronounced as "*YAHWEH*".

The Forever and Highest Order in which the conveyance of the Name of The Father in association to YHWH would be reconciled in Hebrew as "YaHaVah". This was the Name that Yeshua conveyed to His Apostles as the Father's Holy Name.

The letters comprise a word that would transliterate into "*The Sovereign Lord*" or "*The Lord*".

It was so Holy that no one could write or speak it, therefore another word had to be devised which would make up the essence of the transliterated Consonants and could be spoken and used by the common man. This became *ADONAI* (the Lord God).

When the four consonants of **Y** A **H W** E **H** were to be written down in text as Scripture, the word *ADONAI was* used.

Only chosen Scribes from the Tribe of Levi could be the text writer and they had to completely wash themselves each time before scribing the four letters. This is how Holy the Name of God was considered to be viewed as.

Within the 12th to 13th centuries AD, there was a mis-transliteration of the four consonants YHWH and the pronunciation of them used when the Torah was translated into Latin and the YHWH became JHVH and then later translated into German and English, where pronunciation of *YAHWEH* became *Jehovah*.

The 1611 King James transliteration of the complete Torah and Holy Scriptures, TANAKH (Old Testament) and the New Testament incorporated within its published version the mis-transliterated term *Jehovah* where the transcription of the "*The Sovereign Lord*" appeared.

This was later corrected in the New King James Version, commissioned in 1975 by Thomas Nelson Publishers, using 130 respected Bible scholars, church leaders, and lay Christians worked for seven years to create a completely new, modern translation of Scripture, yet one that would retain the purity and stylistic beauty of the original King James English. With unyielding faithfulness to the original Greek, Hebrew, and Aramaic texts, the translation applies the most recent research in archaeology, linguistics, and textual studies.

In this New Version, the term *Jehovah* has been removed and corrected to state, "*The Sovereign Lord*" or the "*Lord God*", as is correct by the original Hebrew text and transliteration as "*ADONAI*".

Jehovah is neither the proper term nor the name of the God of Israel or the Essence of God the Father; and the author has a very strong conviction in not using the mis-transliterated term for the association with the Most High God.

I believe that certain religious orders of the Church love using this term in ignorance, because of standard recognition by Pastors, Evangelists and Teachers, whose formal seminary training were introduced and used the 1611 King James Version of the Bible and believed it to be the literal linguistic translation of the Written Word of God.

The English Church adopted the term *Jehovah* to mean "*The Sovereign Lord*" or "*The Lord*" in replacement of the proper Hebrew

Term of "*ADONAI*" in order to standardize English linguistics and give uniqueness to the term and invoke Cannon Dialect.

Another reason I believe it is so popular amongst certain religious orders is because of a poetic infatuation with the Middle English (Shakespearian) vernacular and the presence of intellectual and scholarly modulation it gives to the speaker.

It also detracts from the one and only Name in which God the Father has given mankind for their Salvation, which is the Name of the Only Begotten Son of God, Yeshua ADONAI, who is "ELOHIM".

In ancient times God would reveal Himself to man in physical manifestations of powerful images, His Shekinah Glory; such as a Burning Bush that spoke to Moses or Fire from Heaven that came in a Roaring Cloud which fell upon Mount Sinai and scorched its top and the ground that Moses stood on, or Miraculous Lightening and the Thunderous Sound of a Voice like a hundred waterfalls, or the image of what looked like the Son of Man sitting in the midst of a fiery furnace too hot for mortal flesh to withstand.

The importance of God establishing His Name with mankind was to give man a means of approaching His Holiness and Grace in receiving both Mercy and Forgiveness in a permanent way through what He would call "*The Word*".

"*The Word*" was in fact one-in-the-same as *ADONAI*, the complete essence of God in Spirit and Being.

It is through "*The Word*" that God Created Everything in existence.

[John 1:1- *"In the beginning was the Word and the Word was with God and the Word <u>was God</u>."*]

[Colossians 1:15-17 - *Christ is the visible image of the invisible God. He existed before anything was created and is supreme over all creation, for through him God created everything in the heavenly realms and on earth. He made the things we can see and the things we can't see—such as thrones, kingdoms, rulers, and authorities in the unseen world. Everything was created through him and for him. He existed before anything else, and he holds all creation together.*]

God finally revealed His Holy and Eternal Name and would sanctify all mankind unto Himself and bridge the gap between death and His Holiness and afford man Eternal Life.

God bridged that gap by sending us "*The Word of God*" in the form of a man (the Son of God - the God Man) who would give us Eternal Life through His Name and be the only sacrifice that would be fulfilling and completely sanctified unto God as a sacrifice worthy of His Sin Offering in accordance with His Law

"*The Word*" becomes flesh and through His Name would be the only source of our forgiveness. (John 1:14-15)

So Holy is His Name, that it is above all things in Heaven and on Earth and in the Underworld; He sits at the Right Hand of the Power of God (The Father) and is the Judge of all mankind.

God has declared that He shall be the Saviour of the world and that His Name is the only source of power which can call upon The Father in fulfilling the Will of God.

The Name of the Son of God is the fulfillment of the 3rd Commandment of God.

The Name of the Son of God is *Yeshua* (Jesus), *Messiah* (The Christ), who is Lord and God (1John 5:19-20).

[Acts 4:11-12 - *For Yeshua is the one referred to in the Scriptures, where it says, 'The stone that you builders rejected has now become the cornerstone. There is salvation in no one else! God has given no other name under heaven by which we must be saved."*]

The Truth that is in God is Holy and has no flaw or lawful interpretation, the Truth through God is Perfect (Pure Light) and guides the pathway of everything in creation from the Throne of God downward to the Earth and mankind.

When Yeshua was standing before Pontius Pilate (the Roman Governor over the province of Judaea) during the judgment trial leading up to His Crucifixion, he told Pilate "*Whoever belongs to the truth listens to me*", then Pilate asked, "And what is truth?" and The Lord remained silent just standing there.

Pilate was looking (face-to-face) at the essence and embodiment of Complete Truth (Who Is, Who Was and Who Is to come again), a preview of what he would face on God's Day of Judgment, when Yeshua will be sitting on the Judgment Seat of God.

The fallout from the Truth is that it exposes a lie.

Truth and a lie don't mix, they can never come together, like oil and water, they cannot congeal into one substance without separating.

It's interesting how one person can speak of a lie and it hits the ears of another and out of deception it can sound like the truth.

In the presence of the Truth a lie becomes a Temptation.

In the Lord's Prayer, the last sentence Jesus states is, "*and lead us not into temptation, but deliver us from Evil (or the <u>Evil One</u>)*." (Matthew 6:13)

This most definitely signifies the true battle between "Good" and "Evil"; between "Righteousness" and "Unrighteousness"; between the "Truth" and a "Lie".

The Evil One is an "Accuser", a "Destroyer", a "Murder and Liar"; where the Lord God is "The Truth", " The Redeemer", "The Creator and Giver of Life".

It's not that God simply Triumphs over evil, for He does in His Abode where there is no evil or anything unrighteous in His Presence; for His Abode in Heaven is just as He is, Holy.

It's that He will eliminate and abolish evil in the physical realm of His Creation, where Satan and the powers of darkness have temporal control over.

Even at that, He still Triumphs over this current element of evil because He has defeated it through the Sacrifice He made on the Cross, while the Son of God (Jesus the Christ) was being crucified and gave His Life as a ransom (He stood in place for us) for the forgiveness of all sin possible and by His death and resurrection He defeated death and the powers of darkness.

Yeshua did what God told Satan He would do to Him in the Garden of Eden during His pronouncing of punishment after Adam had sinned. [Genesis 3:15b - "*Her (Eve's) offspring will crush your head, and you will bite her offspring's heel.*"]

"*Her offspring*" is prophesying to the human lineage of the Man God (Messiah) who would come (the Second Adam) and crush Satan's head and remove his authority and the curse of death through the act of His Sacrifice (Sin Offering) to God.

This is what Yeshua accomplished on the Cross. His sacrifice was the act of clemency that gave us our Salvation and His Resurrection from Death our Eternal Life. [John 14:6 - "*I Am the Way, the Truth and the Life; no one goes to the Father except by me.*"]

As God reveals the Truth to the Church (the collective Body of Christ on Earth) through the Holy Spirit, He uses imperfect vessels (humans) to perform His Perfect Will.

You come to Him just as you are, all filthy with sin, but with a humbled heart ready to receive an Act of Grace and His Perfect Gift, not as a prepared or justified person, all cleaned up and schooled in the ways of religion or performing sacrificial rituals and acts of holiness to prepare yourself worthy to receive His Gift of Salvation.

You can't go to the Seminary to get Saved! You go to the feet of Yeshua on your knees.

God's Power does not come through our abilities to perform anything for Him; His Power is manifested through us once we openly confess a heartfelt recognition that we are a sinner and are completely and totally in need of His Forgiveness because of this reason.

[1John 1:8-9 - *If we say that we have no sin, we are deceiving ourselves and the truth is not in us. If we confess our sins, He is faithful and righteous to forgive us our sins and to cleanse us from all unrighteousness.*]

This verse of Scripture is not referring to the Believers in Christ having to constantly confess that we are sinners to the Lord but refers to the one time when a person finally realizes that they are born with sin and are claiming God's act of Forgiveness and Clemency through the shed Blood of Yeshua and His death on the Cross.

For it is by this single act of the Lord to poise Himself as the Lamb of God and die for the complete and total remission of all sins, that each and every person is forgiven whether they receive Yeshua or not.

His Life was given for ALL Mankind once and for all and has made Forgiveness of Sin available to everyone whether they receive and acknowledge it or not.

Everyone is Forgiven and there is nothing that any human being can do to be unforgiven.

His Forgiveness covers the Law and stands as the proxy over the sins we've committed in the past, present or future...<u>ALL</u> of Us!

Salvation and Eternal Life with God is another thing. Salvation is different than being Forgiven.

We need Forgiveness because of what Adam did in the Garden of God and became sin because of his act of disobedience and blasphemy.

That removed the Holy Spirit out of the man and passed down a dead spirit through birth to all of mankind from that point forward.

The Forgiveness of God was necessary first in order that we may then receive His Salvation. God's Forgiveness does not Save you.

Unless you tap into God's Salvation and receive Yeshua ADONAI (Jesus the Lord) as God you are not saved!

Once you commit that heartfelt act of openly (with your mouth) confessing your need for God's Saving Grace and believe it from your heart through your mind, then you are Saved (Romans 10:9-13), otherwise, your sins have been forgiven, but your name will not be written into the Lambs Book of the Living ("Book of Life"). How sad it is to think that everyone is forgiven of all their sins before God, but until they confess that Yeshua ADONAI and believe that in their heart and spirit, they will not receive that Salvation nor be put into the Book of the Living. They will go into the Final Judgement, and they have already condemned themselves to the Lake of Fire and eternal Damnation. It was their decision!

It is by His Grace and Mercy that we receive our Salvation and the Gift of Eternal Life and not because of any act that we have performed in order to bring about our own Salvation.

[<u>Ephesians 2:9</u> - "*Salvation is not a reward for the good things we have done, so none of us can boast about it.*"]

We have to be "*Born Again*" Yeshua said in order to see the Kingdom of God (John 3:1-8).

We were all born into this world by the act of human reproduction under Gods creative order, but because God has created us in His Image (Spirit) we also have an Eternal Image within us that must be considered, which is our sinful and dead human spirit.

This is where the change and transformation occur within us, as we are given a rebirth through the Spirit once we receive this Grace of Salvation from our heartfelt repentance and can openly confess that Jesus (Yeshua) is Lord and God! [Romans 10:10 - "*For it is with your heart that you believe and are justified, and it is with your mouth that you profess your faith (in Jesus the Christ) and are saved.*"]

It is our spirit which is "*Born Again*" as it transforms from being dead into becoming alive!

Once again, this is what was taken from Adam when he sinned and it is important to reiterate this truth, that God had brought man from a molded image of the dust of the earth and breathed His Holy Spirit into it and Man became a Living Being (Genesis 2:7), but when Man volunteered to be disobedient against God's Word and Command, the Lord God imposed His judgment against the sin the man had committed and He retracted the Holy Spirit from mankind and death filled his spirit and he became a indigent creature and a walking Dead Man. (Genesis 3:19)

This is the True Part of us that lives forever, our spirit, which is either dead and destined to the grave and judgment or alive and in the Presence of the Living God.

Either way, it is Eternal (time without end) and there are only two choices.

God Himself gives us a New Name and writes our name in His Book of the Living (also known as the Book of Life).

This is a very good thing considering the outcome of not having your name written in His Book. [Revelation 20:14-15 - "*Then death and Hades were thrown into the lake of fire. The lake of fire is the second death. Anyone whose name was not found written in the Book of Life was thrown into the Lake of Fire.*"]

The secular misconception of the Judeo-Christian God is that He is perceived as vengeful (even hateful), an over-lording tyrant who is ready to damn you and scorn you with Lightning Bolts and Fire and Brimstone.

The abstract paintings and images from secular artists trying to influence and conjure up the essence of God's Fury against mankind is always showing the Wrath of God, where an angel of God is throwing people into the Bottomless Pit or Hell where they pile up on top of each other.

A place where there is fire and smoke and hungry demons with sharp teeth and long spiky claws waiting to tear into their flesh and torment them.

There are horrible images of these demons eating and chewing on people, having sex with them and causing all sorts of mayhem.

These were scare tactics conjured up by the Roman Catholic Church during the Middle-Ages and through the Protestant Reformation Church in Europe during the 16th and 17th Centuries, meant to put the Fear of God into a person and keep the Faithful-Faithful and control their loyalty towards the Church and its respective dogmas.

People had little reference to the Bible or the Scriptures during these times, since hard copies were not in mass publication as they have been since the late 19th and 20th Centuries into our present day; and illiteracy was prevalent, so reliance on the church leadership or seminary scholars to minister and interpret the Written Word of God in accordance with individually defined religious doctrine or the pictorial hieroglyphics is all there was for the commoner (layperson).

This followed by strict rituals and fearful propaganda kept the masses under Canon Law (ecclesiastical authority) and aided to control the social and political order of not only the Christian Church, but many of the world's governments.

It still exists within the Body of Christ to this day, where fear is used to convict and control how the Faithful stay faithful to a common cause or united religious consortium and social order.

It seems that fear has always been our most primal and instinctive emotion and has more profound effects on our human psyche than happiness does.

Fear becomes overwhelming and causes panic and chaos and makes us think and react irrationally, which is enhanced physically due to our prevalent sin nature and the environment of a deprived world (fallen state of humanity) that we are constantly exposed to.

It's prevalent enough that God mentions for us "Not to Fear" (in some form or another) 365 times throughout the Bible.

Fear is the enemy of Faith and births Doubt, which is the sinful element of Fear.

Our five physical senses are the only point of reality for most people, including faithful Christians, that what we can see and feel is more overwhelming than just having blind faith in something that is not physically substantial.

It takes no faith to fear, it is a reactionary human emotion stemming from our Sin Nature, but it takes Complete Faith in God not to fear; that when something is attacking your physical being and is confirmed by your five physical senses, means you have to stand in resisting what is seen by something that is unseen. [Hebrews 11:1 - "*Now faith is the assurance that what we hope for will come about and the certainty that what we cannot see exists.*"]

With all of this said, we must also conclude that the "Word of God" (Yeshua ADONAI) and the Testimony within the Written Word of God (the Holy Bible) most definitely pronounces and defines a place of death (the Grave or in Hebrew-Sheol) where those that die with a dead spirit, who are not "*Born Again*" are held while waiting for the Great and Terrible Day of the Lord, the Final Judgment of God. (Revelation 20:11-15) - I have more to say about this and the Lake of Fire at the end of this book under "*An Open and Personal Testimony*".

This is not what some think to be Purgatory, as is exasperated in the Catholic doctrine as a holding place in the afterlife between Heaven and Hell, in order for the person to overcome their shortfalls in this life by spiritual existential examination and working out the remainder of unaccounted sin before either being welcomed into Heaven or thrown into the Eternal Fire.

In the Gospel of Luke, the 16th Chapter, verses 19-31, Yeshua gave an example of the final outcome when a person departs from this life and enters into the eternal spirit or next life waiting the Final Day of Judgment.

There is a holding place which God had devised for the wicked and unsaved which is separated from the Love of God, a place called the World of the Dead or Sheol.

In this example of Lazarus and the Rich Man, it shows a great chasm which separates those who have died and are in the Bosom of Abraham and those who are dead and in Hades.

That once we die, the outcome of our eternal decision that we made while alive on this earth has been sealed and there is no more repentance or "Turning Back".

In this example what Lazarus is witnessing was the "then" current state of Spiritual Damnation before Jesus had suffered Death and Risen from the Grave. This place within the bowels of the earth called Hades is no longer occupied now that Jesus has risen from the dead and sits at the Right Hand of God on the Mercy Seat of Salvation.

That during his 3 days of death, He (Yeshua) went to Hades and redeemed the lost there and they either followed him to Paradise in Heaven or were departed to Sheol.

Sheol is currently a Dark and Cold Place of torment for those who are waiting the Day of Judgement, the other place that has been created is the Lake of Fire, which is currently empty and waiting for Satan and the Powers of Darkness, as well as the outcome of the Judgement that Christ will put forth on the Day of Judgement for those who will forever be cast into.

"*God is Love*" and He is Righteous in all of His Manner and Revelation to the Church through the Holy Spirit, but He is also Justice and unwavering towards sin regarding the outcome of punishment He has pronounced against it. [Romans 6:23 - "*For the wages of sin is death, but the gift of God is eternal life in Christ Jesus our Lord.*"]

Damnation is not the Will of God for any of us and is not the result of His Nature or the resounding characteristic of His dominate

Virtues (Faith, Hope and Love). [2Peter 3:9 - "*The Lord is not slack concerning His promise, as some men count slackness, but is patient toward us, not willing that any should perish, but that all should come to repentance (and be saved)*"]

Nevertheless, His Holiness and Righteous Justice demands total and complete accountability and Judgment against sin in order to eradicate it forever.

The testimony that will stand before God in doing this are the Books of Accountability and the witness will be the Bride of Christ (the Resurrected Church).

The Great White Throne Judgment of God is the Final Act of Justice before all things in the creation are brought in line to the complete fulfillment of God's Holiness and Substantiation.

Yeshua is presently sitting on the Mercy Seat in the Holy of Holies in the Presence of God the Father acting as the Advocate of all who called upon His Name for their Salvation, pronouncing us sinless before the Father and receiving the heartfelt prayers of repentant souls and allowing them to enter into the Kingdom of God and be written into the Lambs Book of the Living (receiving Salvation Evermore).

This was represented in the Holy Temple when it was on earth in Jerusalem.

The tenth day of the seventh month" (Tishrei), regarded as the "Sabbath of Sabbaths", is designated as the Day of Atonement (Yom Kippur).

On that day, the Holy Presence of God (His Shekinah), in the form of a cloud, would hover above the complex of the Tabernacle during the time of Moses in the desert and the Temple when it was in Jerusalem.

When the proper acts of preparation and Blood Offerings had been completed in accordance to the Law of Moses, the High Priest would enter into the Holy of Holies where the Arc of the Covenant was; and he would sprinkle the Blood of the Lamb (Atonement Sacrifice) on the Kapporet (the Golden Cover or Seat of the Arc of the Covenant), then the Presence of the Lord God would fall upon the Tabernacle / Temple and appear within the Holy of Holies as the Image of the Son of Man seated on the Kapporet to receive the Sin Offering and forgive the Sins of the Nation for another year; then the Cloud of the Holy Presence of God would be retracted back unto Heaven.

In the Final Judgment (Great White Throne Judgment-Revelation 20:11-15), Yeshua will be sitting on the Judgment Seat of God, Books will be opened (all of the Books of Human Accountability) and another Book, the Book of the Living.

Anyone not found in the Book of the Living will be judged according to what they have done against the Standard of the Law which God has established.

Everyone found to be in the Book of the Living will be judged and found Not Guilty of any account against the Law because their Salvation has been given to them by their Faith in receiving Jesus as their Lord and Savior and are under the Blood Covenant of His Sacrifice; they became "*Born Again*" by the Holy Spirit and at the moment they repented and made that heartfelt confession unto His Name, their names were written in the Lambs Book of the Living.

It's one thing to have our sins forgiven of us (Past, Present and Forever) as we look to the Cross of His Crucifixion; but Salvation comes by the heartfelt confession of repentance that we are sinners and in need of God's free gift through His Grace and Mercy.

It's when we receive Jesus as Lord and God to be our Savior and we transform from a dead spirit inside of us to a reborn "Living Spirit" inside of us.

When Yeshua said on the cross, "*It Is Finished!*" and gave up His Spirit to the Father, God was at that moment completely and forever satisfied with the fulfillment of the Levitical Law and the Atonement Offering.

At that moment the Curtain (Veil) in the Holy Temple which separated the Holy of Holies and the Holy Place, was torn in half from top to bottom; signifying that God was no longer separating man from entering into His Presence (Holy of Holies) and that the High Priest was no longer needed on Earth but would now be seated at the Right Hand of Almighty God as our Advocate and Saviour.

[Hebrews 10:17-21 - *And then He (Yeshua) said, "I will not remember their sins and evil deeds any longer." So, when these have been forgiven, an offering to take away sins is no longer needed. We have, then, my friends, complete freedom to go into the Most Holy Place by means of the death of Yeshua. He opened for us a new way, a living way, through the curtain - That is, through His own Body. We have a Great Priest in charge of the House of God.*]

All of the Law (the full extent of the Law) was no longer necessary in order to give temporal satisfaction to Appease God's Anger (Wrath) against sin and Man's sinful nature; thus, Temporal Atonement as directed by the Law was no longer necessary, for now God had given Propitiation to sin through the Permanent Atonement and Blood Sacrifice of the Only Begotten Son of God (Jesus the Christ). *"It Is Finished!"* meant "It Is Over!", Now and Forever!

* * * * * *

Do you ever feel that God is totally against you or not part of your life any longer?

That He may have rethought Himself about Forgiving you and you have fallen from His Grace due to your inability to uphold the statutes of the Law and Commandments given in the Bible.

That everything you attempt somehow gets side-tracked away from you and only bad things prosper in your life, more so now than before you accepted Yeshua (Jesus) as your Lord and Savior.

That every prayer you ask of God falls on a deaf ear.

Or maybe you feel you're not worthy for God to answer your prayers; maybe you haven't done enough good things or you're still a sinner and you just can't stop doing the bad things you did before you came to the Christ and that is why He has distanced Himself from you.

There's a lot of reasons Christians start feeling unworthy when they can't maintain that euphoric feeling and experience, they first had when receiving Jesus into their hearts and felt that rebirth of their soul come to life.

As the trials and tribulations that you experienced before you came to Christ start to come back into your life, your Christian Walk becomes challenging, and you may not understand how God would let this happen to you.

I mean, you're under the Blood of Christ now and all the demons and bad things are supposed to flee from you; only good things are supposed to happen now that you're a Christian, Right?

It's sad to think that this is the mindset and reality for so many individuals who have put their Trust and Faith in Yeshua ADONAI and carry with then the label as "A Child of God".

You believe the Bible is the Truth, you have read it (or at least been spoon fed in church) and believe it to be the Inspired Word of God; and if you're a church goer, it is the very book that is used by your Pastor as the source of all Truth and Christian Ministry.

You know and have confessed that Jesus has Forgiven you of all your sins and that you have Everlasting Life through your Faith in Him; but it's all Pie in the Sky when it comes down to Earth for you personally, when trials and tribulations begin happening.

You would expect as much in the life of the non-Believer (someone who doesn't believe in Jesus), where their daily existence is a Crapshoot, like throwing the dice of your desires and wishes on the Big Cosmic Crap Table of Chance and hoping for Good Luck and Good Fortune to be bestowed upon you.

In so many instances people (even Christians) give themselves all the praise and credit when you win, but when you lose it's an empty disappointment with no hope or guidance for recovery and usually God gets the blame for your failures; everything is reliant on the individual making their own destiny, reaching for the highs and recovering from the lows which follow you down life's rocky pathway towards inevitable death, with the prize being the proclamation that, "the One who dies with the most…<u>Wins!</u>"

I've had a few moments in my life where I've prayed to the Lord for something, and the answer or request was manifested almost immediately, and you know beyond doubt that it was something so impossible for anyone to do except God Himself.

I can't tell you how wonderful it feels to have that happen; it seems like you are so close to God and that you have so much favor with Him. It boosts your Faith to an all-time high.

It's such a supernatural experience that you ponder on the circumstance leading up to it, trying to see if there was a pattern you may have done to bring about such a faithful event, like you may have found the right formula that pleases God in answering your requests.

Then the next time you come before the Lord with another desperate request, and you pray so hard, but this time He is not so quick to answer the request and a bad thing happens, just the opposite of what you were hoping for and even in some cases, your worst nightmare.

It seems like you're tossing a coin in the air calling, "Heads you win, Tails you lose!"

For myself, I always go back to the one verse of Scripture that I believe with all of my heart is true, but a mystery in that it is not always done on my timing; and Jesus said to them, "*Very truly I tell you, whoever believes in me will do the works I have been doing, and they will do even greater things than these, because I am going to the Father. And I will do whatever you ask in my name, so that the Father may be glorified in the Son.* If you ask anything in My Name, I will do it. (John 14:12-13)

For Father God purposes all things according to His Will.

As a Child of God, the pathway in this life is not always going to be traveled in the direction I purpose it to be but will always be to my benefit in recognizing that I am a Child of God, a rightful heir to His Kingdom and that He does Love me, far above anything or anyone could ever do.

We have to reconcile the fact, that if we believe in God through Christ Jesus, then we must surrender it all to Him, Body, Soul and Spirit. We cannot help Him help us.

That Faith prevails and doubt is cast aside, and our entire point of worship is God and everything we do relies on His Wisdom and Spirit to guide us.

Faith through Christ does not require that we achieve any level of enlightenment, transcendence, or ultra-consciousness to achieve absolute human perfection, but rather that we surrender to the Will of God through the Word of God. [Romans 10:17 - "*for Faith comes by hearing and hearing by the Word of God.*"]

The Lord told us that we would suffer Trials and Tribulations in this life, not in order to beat us down and keep us under His control, but rather that we may endure through His Strength and Grace, holding onto nothing but Him and learning to rely on His Power to perfect us out of a sin nature and sin conscientiousness into a Faithful remnant of His Nature and Holiness.

In the midst of the pain, we suffer through the Trials and Tribulation, God sends us Joy to encourage us.

God does not bring us Joy to remove the pain of suffering these things, but in order to endure it.

It's a constant tearing down and building up process of our refinement with bringing us under submission to the Will of God in our lives.

The flesh does not want to Praise God and neither does our dead human spirit which is inherent within us at birth.

We are constantly at battle within ourselves (the flesh) to judge what is good and what is bad and to resist what is evil and accept the righteous path in our moment-by-moment existence.

The fortitude in doing this is through Faith, Faith in Jesus the Christ, who has won the battle for us on the Cross and stands as our Advocate before Father God, proclaiming that we belong to Him, and the Spirit gives testimony to this, in that God has written our names in the Lambs Book of the Living.

It is important to remember that all who receive Yeshua as their Lord and Savior have their names written in the Lambs book of the Living and the Book of Life.

* * * * * *

One of the most controversial and exploited events of the Modern Evangelical Protestant Movement, has been anticipating the occurrence of what is known as the (Taking Away) or "Rapture of the Church". It has been associated to the Last Days of the End-Times of the Christian Church and marked as the last of seven (7) dispensational periods of the Church Age (Time of the Gentiles) known as the Church of Laodicea (Lukewarm). Mentioned by the Apostle John in the New Testament Book of Revelation 3:14-21 and described in detail as to how it will occur in manner and circumstance by the Apostle Paul in two letters to the Corinthian and Thessalonian churches (1Corinthians 15:50-54 and 1Thessalonians 4:13-18). Paul was not speaking about a timeline to a particular Dispensational Period through these verses, but rather a supernatural event that God would bring about in purging the earth of "The Elect" (God's Chosen Ones - Body of Christ) which would include all of the dead in Christ and the current living who are in Christ. The timeline of this actual event is identified in the Book of Revelation 14:14-16 just before the Bowl Judgements (Bowls of God's Wrath) would be poured out on the earth, just after the Abomination of Desolation occurs, starting the Great Tribulation (Revelation 16:1-16). Up until this point, God's Wrath has not come against the earth and mankind to this extent of manifesting such Great Tribulation in all of human existence. There is a promise from ADONAI that we (The Elect) shall not suffer such Wrath from God in any manner, that our suffering of any kind of tribulation shall only come from our existence in this world, but we shall not suffer His Wrath as the world is going to in this manner (1Thessalonians 5:9-15).

We have without doubt already gone through the Final Dispensational Period of the Church Age (Laodicea) and have now entered into the beginnings of the Minor Tribulation Period. I have put together a TimeLine, which highlights the events starting with the First Advent of Christ, (His Birth-Ministry-Death and Resurrection-Ascension), through the Church Age, periods of the 7-year Tribulation, point at which the Rapture occurs, His Second Advent, and His 1000 Year Reign on earth. I must be explicitly clear that this is not a prophecy as a Dateline of events (Matthew 24:36), but rather a Time-Line of past history and what I believe ADONAI has given me in foresight as to what is going forward through the Period known as "The Tribulation", and mark the time period in which the Rapture of the Church will occur.

What the Lord God (ADONAI) has shown me, is that the Church (Collective Body of Believers) Dead and Living, will not be resurrected (Raptured) in a Pre-Trib, Mid-Trib or Post-Trib manner, but rather we will witness and go through all of the manner and events of the Tribulation up to the Abomination of Desolation, and then sometime between that event and the beginning of God pouring out His Anger and Wrath upon the earth and mankind, the Rapture will occur. "But he that shall endure to the end, the same shall be saved" (Matthew 24:13).

This is a Mystery that is not to be shared with the Body of Christ, thus if Jesus had insight to it from the Father, then He would tell us (the Church) through the Holy Spirit who reveals everything that is in the preview of the Son, who is One with the Father; but with this event, the Father is restraining foresight through the Son and keeping it from the Church for His purpose.

Jesus did however reveal what the Father set forth in regard to the Church Age and "Signs of the Times" which would be fulfilled in the Last Days of the "End Times", prior to the Rapture of the Church.

It is the last of the prophetic events before the Tribulation would begin and God's Wrath would come upon the Earth to Judge this world. (Matthew 24:29-31, Revelation 6:1-17)

So how are we, the Elite in Christ (His Body) supposed to act while ministering to a rampaged and faithless world.

It must be done in Boldness and in Faith which is given through Love, but not in fear of persecution or retribution, least The Lord receives no Glory for our actions.

We must realize that in Christ we are His Children and at the same time, we are to be His Servants to both one another and to the Gospel.

Jesus said, *"Blessed are the meek for they shall inherit the earth."* (Matthew 5:5).

Many religious people give the wrong interpretation to the context of what Jesus was meaning here and teach that the term "Meek" meant being "Timid or Reserved" (non-aggressive).

Some religious scholars go so far as to say this line of Scripture demonstrates the true meaning of being "Christ-Like", that to be a true Follower of Christ you should never show any act of aggressive manner and always have a show of Peace and Love in your demeanor, like Jesus did.

This is a perfect example where the Christian should be aware that the Truth is being circumvented by using partial truth and human reasoning to conjure up a deceptive lie.

This is where the powers of darkness and the Evil One love using our human self-righteousness against the Power that God has given us in Christ Jesus.

The true meaning behind the word "Meek" as used by The Lord in this context, meant "Humble in Faith", and this in-turn means remaining in Faith and Resisting Evil.

We as the Redeemed in Christ, His Body where the Holy Spirit resides, shall not be Timid towards Evil, but have Faith in Resisting it through the Word of God and our Testimony of the Truth.

Even though something looks good from our human perspective, if it is not guided by the Word of God or the Will of God and is the provision of an evil source, then we are to rebuke it and even Hate It.

[Psalm 11:5-6 - *"The Lord tests the righteous, but his soul hates the wicked... On the wicked he will rain fiery coals and burning sulfur; a scorching wind will be their lot."*]

There should be nothing passive or timid about how we as Christians react to evil or the unrighteousness of those who reject Yeshua ADONAI as Lord and God.

We (The Body of Christ) are His Witness to the truth, for in each and every one of us is the Holy Spirit, who gives all truth about The Lord and the Will of God.

It is through us in Faith that we give the Testimony of Truth that Yeshua ADONAI (Jesus is Lord); no one else, other than the Body of Christ has this truth in their message and no one else reveals the source of any truth without this message, whose Source is the Holy Spirit of God Almighty.

This is not to condemn what is Good, for Good is Good and Bad is Bad and Evil is Evil; but it is to say that there is NOTHING anyone of us can do towards doing enough Good Deeds or Good Things to fulfill the Law or the Commandments of the Bible.

It is only by Faith in Christ Jesus that we receive our Salvation and our Testimony of Truth, and the Power given to us by the Holy Spirit in order to pronounce it!

The Law and Good Deeds do nothing to redeem or save anyone; it never has, and it never will!

The biggest lie and deception that the powers of darkness and the Evil One conjure up in the minds of weak and unfaithful Christians is that they need to stop sinning and turn towards passive peace and stop confronting evil aggressively.

That if we just turn the other cheek and show love towards evil, then we will overcome the evil thing through goodness, even if it overtakes and kills you, then God will be pleased with the outcome of your actions.

Nothing could be farther from the truth!

While we are still on this Earth, the only source of resistance to evil is the individual Believer in Christ and the Church collective as a Body.

In the Written Word of God there is more context towards how Yeshua rebuked evil with Hands-On Commands and physical contact than any passive show of love towards it.

You don't have to get into a fight with evil, but you need to get physically Faithful in Rebuking it...You have to Hate It (the Evil Thing) as much as you Love God, because love towards God means that you hate what is evil and will not partake in what they do and admonish the wicked thing.

The misconception of the "Turn the other cheek" phrase that Jesus was speaking of in the Book of Matthew, Chapter 5 verse 39 is not to be timid or submissive towards evil, but to not allow the evil thing to retract you from projecting the Power of Christ through your Testimony of the Truth through Peace with Love.

Love in this context is not a show of passionate embrace or a thankful kiss; it is the show of strong rebuke in a manner of steadfastness towards your Love for God and what is Righteous.

It was meant to show how we are to conduct ourselves when approached by aggressive people, who while we are giving our testimony of the Truth about Salvation through Christ want to intimidate us through either physical force or aggressive physical resistance.

If we partake in response to the same aggressive force while giving our testimony, then we fail to project what our testimony of Truth is saying.

But, in every situation where evil is pronounced, we are to rebuke it with all of our being, in complete and total Faith without Doubt, and God will prevail against it and be Glorified through our Testimony which is what the Holy Spirit has given us to pronounce.

It is God and God alone who is the Truth!

CHAPTER IV
(God is the Creator of all Truth)

"The Dawning of Creation" is a mystical term and thought, which expresses the essence of how unknowingly we understand our existence.

Its abstract compromise is based on the illusion that the human mind has preeminence over factual data which supports the physical content of the complete and visible universe.

The pretense is that if you can tap deep enough into the inner power of your psyche and focus your mantra energy towards infinite channeling, then you can produce kinetic energy and create physical manifestations without mechanical induction, such as bend a piece of metal or start a fire through spontaneous combustion or even levitate and move physical items.

This form of incantation has been known throughout centuries past as "Witchcraft", but in modern times carries a newer label known as "Mind over Matter".

What is actually occurring, is getting a little help from your demonic friends, who are the force behind the physical manifestations.

The psyche and mantra energy being "channeled" is a term which means "summoning" and actually calling upon the powers of darkness to force your will to be done; but hanging out with that crowd is not free, there is always a price to be paid and one that can never be "Paid in Full". You end up giving up the precious gift that God the Creator has given to you, Your Life! And to something that absolutely despises and hates your very existence.

Evolutionists believe that the universe has always existed and evolves through hyper-changes which have no planned or organized intelligence motivating it; that our own existence was by chance through a primordial mixture of chemicals and elements coming together at random coincidence to form the elementary organisms that have evolved into the state of all current life-forms, which exist and will continue to evolve to higher and higher life forms.

Reincarnation attempts to rationalize a beginning or start of the life experience to a revolving door of random rebirth and recycling of the life event to reaching a utopian platform of the ultra-spiritual existence and highest level of Human Enlightenment and Being into entering "Eternal Being" (out of body existence).

This would achieve the highest possible evolutionary state that one's being can aspire to and give them eternal life outside of their physical state of existence.

Existentialism is the belief that existence precedes essence, which means that the most important consideration for an individual is that they are "an individual", anatomic and separate from any joining life force or spirit.

It is not uncommon for individuals who believe in the theories of existentialism to have a condition called an "Existential Crisis", which are super-psychotic moments where an individual seriously questions the very foundations of their life (whether their life has any meaning, purpose, or value).

This condition produces uncertainty regarding faith in exercising the individual's ability to control their own environment and surroundings, which usually will manifest into psychotic events such as paranoia, delusion, manic depression and even suicide if becoming chronic.

Whether you're a Concept Creationist believing that all things came into existence out of nothing in a trillionth, of a trillionth, of a second through the "Big Bang", or you're a Biblical Creationist believing that God brought all things into existence out of nothing instantaneously and molded the entire universe and the Earth with all of the life forms on it (including Man) as we know it literally within six earth days; the fact is that at the moment of existence (Creation) "Time" began.

The Jewish Torah and Talmud make references to "since the beginning of time" or "since time began", which indicates that time did have a beginning and that time has not always been in existence.

The bible refers to God as having No Beginning and No End (Eternal).

Yeshua is referred to as the "Alpha" and "Omega"; the "Beginning" and the "End". (Revelation 1:8)

Within the creation of substance, time was also part of that, existing in parallel and subsequently moving through space and expelling energy and motion.

The Biblical Creationist believes that God created all life forms, both in Heaven and in the physical universe (on Earth) for a purpose that Glorifies Him and simultaneously fulfills His Will through all that He has created.

The Concept Creationist doesn't really care who did what, just that all things in the universe are the result of some cataclysmic event "Big Bang" that has a center point of beginning, how it came about is a mystery and open to scientific discovery.

All time, just as all physical matter and energy, has a calculated expenditure of existence and life.

This is why time as we know it in the physical realm does not exist in the Presence of God where Eternity is (Time Without End).

Atheists have no belief in creation as having a beginning or an end or that anything has evolved or coexisted.

All matter and existence is what it is, "here and now" and that science is relative only in achieving a higher human platform of current existence.

Once you are born, which occurs due to the human reproductive engine and the act of sexual intercourse, there is a space of undetermined time that you physically live and at some point, you will cease to exist (die) and at that state all physical consciousness and life existence ends.

Ever talk to an atheist to try and find out what it is they really believe in?

In my adult life experience, I've known quite a few atheists and actually befriended one for a few years; and what I've found are self-centered, self-absorbed and selfish individuals, in total disregard of others, who are confused about every aspect of life and are only willing to listen to what their itchy ears want to hear at the moment.

In bold and arrogant mannerism, they claim no belief in anything (meaning spiritual or religious), but in reality, they believe in anything that sounds good to feed their sinful nature.

The truth is, deep down inside they are the most insecure and frightened people you'll ever meet.

Their insecurity shows in outward arrogance, rude behavior and boastful blasphemy against God basically because they hate all authority.

They usually need to be an overachiever or activist in some radical movement or purpose that makes them forget about what happens to you when your life comes to an end as if they are constantly rebelling and trying to shock you with their big mouths and sinful conduct.

The old atheist mantra, "Eat, Drink and be Merry, for tomorrow we shall die" is all hyperbole, for you can believe that they don't want to die any more than anyone else does.

There's an old military saying, "There are no atheists in the foxhole" and in most every instance when a person is confronted with the overwhelming reality that death is just upon them, there is an instigative fear that bellows out of the human spirit that calls out to God for His Saving Grace to spare their life.

People will promise God anything just to save their life, then later recant it when all is well.

Atheists like going after the easy Christian religions like Presbyterians, Protestants, Catholics, Baptists, Evangelicals, who approach their blasphemy and outlandish hatred of God with love and forgiveness hoping that they can be converted.

You won't find them going after Islam or the Muslim Faith for the fear and knowledge that they will be killed in some gruesome fashion and Islam will not stand for open atheism, rude conduct or perverts that commit homosexuality.

They like to classify themselves as humanists, but with a burning passion for pleasures and the good things this life can afford them. They 'Want" but are not willing to "Give".

It's all about the "Corporate Good" of mankind.

They're the first to get behind any Self-Righteous cause that promotes Human Rights which embrace liberal organizations that appear to be caring for human life but are the first to deny the rights of an unborn child to life if the mother wants to murder it in the womb.

They'll fight to the death for an animal to have the same rights as a human but will not protest for the Right to Life and against the mass murdering of hundreds and thousands of children within abortion clinics.

They have a fervent hatred towards anyone expressing their belief in God (especially Christians or the Gospel of Christ) and make it their agenda to withhold the rights of others to freely do so by using the law as a weapon of oppression.

These people are all liars and do not have the Truth in them, for The Lord condemns them for their blasphemy and gives His favor towards His Children, for The Lord declares, *"No weapon that is formed against you shall prosper; and every tongue that shall rise against you in judgment you shall condemn. This is the heritage of the servants of the LORD, and their righteousness is of me, thus says the LORD"* (Isaiah 54:17)

"Therefore, God exalted him to the highest place and gave him the name that is above every name, that at the name of Yeshua every knee should bow, in heaven and on earth and under the earth, and every tongue confess that Yeshua ADONAI, to the glory of God the Father." (Philippians 2:9-11)

The purpose of the Gospel of Christ is not to convert anyone to Christianity or any Religious Order, but to give a fallen world and a sinful human race the Conditions of Salvation and the Good News that "Our Captivity to Sin, is Over!", and that God has opened a door that cannot be closed to all people for the Forgiveness of their Sins and a pathway of Righteousness to those who want to be saved and obtain Everlasting Life.

Even while Yeshua walked the earth, He was eradicating the very foundation that sin was continually destroying.

Through healing of sick and diseased bodies, rebuking evil spirits out of people and of course the ultimate through raising the dead, God's first and foremost purpose for His Visitation was the Remission and Forgiveness of Sin and to give mankind the True and Everlasting pathway to Eternal Life through Yeshua.

No other god or deity, can or will, fulfill the promise of Salvation to Eternal Life and the Forgiveness of Sin other than the proclaimed One and True God, Jesus of Nazareth (**Yeshua HaMashiach**).

[1John 5:20 - *And we know that the Son of God has come and has given us an understanding, that we may know Him who is true; and we are in Him who is true, in His Son Jesus the Christ. This is the true God and Eternal Life.*]

* * * * * *

It is indeed an awesome experience to be living in the Last Days of the End-Times.

As I read through the Bible and try to understand what the people of those times were believing regarding the coming of the "End of the Age" that Yeshua spoke of, I realize that the majority of them thought that the events being prophesied would happen during their lifetime.

Two millenniums later, we realize that we are that last generation which shall not perish before the Lord returns for His Church.

We think of how blessed those people were during the time of Yeshua and what they witnessed and saw, but now we are actually living during the days that Yeshua and the Prophets spoke of as the End-Times.

ADONAI prophesied in the 24th Chapter of the Book of Matthew, both physical and social events that would take place on earth as part of the Signs of the Times, revealing the approach of the final hours (meaning the months or years) before the Church would be taken out of this world.

One of the most frightening prophecies is the impending persecution of the Church world-wide and a falling away. [Matthew 24: 9-10 - *Then you (Christians) will be arrested and handed over to be punished and be put to death. Everyone will hate you because of me. Many will give up their faith at that time; they will betray one another and hate one another.*]

It seems beyond belief that in this moment in time, we are witnessing the all-out "massive" persecution of Christians around the world, even unto death, but this is only the beginning, The persecution and upheavals that Christians are going to go through shall be even greater as we go through the timeline of events of the Minor and Major Tribulation period. It is not until we (the Church) witness the Abomination of Desolation that we are taken out of this earth as a collective body (the Church), then what will follow is the Great Tribulation then the end of the Age.

It is important to note that Yeshua made mention of the Church being persecuted as a major event which would point to the "End of the Age" as being very near.

The major and most compelling reason it is occurring in this generation is because of the unbelievable upswing in the Muslim Islamic religion around the world.

God is unleashing in these Last Days of the End-Times, extreme and powerful demonic forces that have been restrained since the beginning of the world, to come forth now and fulfill the prophecies that were foretold and bring about His Righteous Judgment against the depravity that man has brought about on the earth, even greater than Sodom and Gomorrah.

The murderous creed of the Islamic religion is the perfect vehicle to deliver the evil agenda of the powers of darkness.

The Muslim community and Islamic religion have for decades been projecting itself as peaceful and very religious, to the extent that they will not tolerate any outside customs or religion to interfere with their demand to worship according to the strict laws of the Qur'an.

They are and have always been fanatics in keeping the order their religious laws and dedication to their Prophet Mohammad and their god Allah.

This dedication to Allah makes them warriors and their dedication to the Qur'an makes them murderers at heart.

In these Last Days, the secular and social depravity of the human race through perverted lifestyles and immoral acts, along with the exploding influence of terrorist religious fanatics are feeding an ever-growing fire of rebellion against God and aiding the demonic forces behind them to strengthen their position within all human societies.

It is unbelievable that the United States of America could ever embrace the persecution of Christianity or lawfully go after the message of Jesus the Christ as being a hateful religious doctrine, but that is exactly what happened under the Liberal Progressive Movement of the Obama Administration in 2014.

It started back in early 1960's in America when atheists were able to outlaw Christian Prayer in our public schools, citing the separation of Church and State under the U.S. Constitution.

The reality is that there is <u>NO</u> mention or reprove regarding separation of Church and State anywhere within the United States Constitution!

In fact, the opposite is true. We have under the U.S. Constitution, the Right of Religious Freedom; to openly without restriction, practice whatever religion we chose to under the protection of the law.

It's a made-up restriction that the God-Haters of our society invoked without even one member of the U.S. Congress or the Supreme Court rebuking it as illegal.

What was cited was a misquoted comment that Thomas Jefferson made in a paper he wrote after the Declaration of Independence was drafted; where he said, 'that we would want to separate any one religious order from becoming the implemented doctrine of faith to the United States", like so many countries had at that time in Europe (i.e.; France, Spain, Italy, England), where the Church (in this case the Roman Catholic Church) was imposed within the government as both law and dogma.

What's even more unbalanced is that with the atheistic move to replace Christian Prayer in our public schools, a more secular religious doctrine, called "Evolution", took its place.

A Godless lie that rebukes any essence of the Creator in a shroud of scientific misconceptions.

Even the creator of the concept, Charles Darwin, retracted his own stance regarding it later in his life.

After he was able to reanalyze and rethink it, he concluded that the theorem was unsubstantiated in both fact and science.

Even he could not believe it any longer; but once out there the secular humanists and non-God believing science community would never let it die.

It would become their model for explaining the biggest lie ever conceived.

[Matthew 24:11-12 - *Then many false prophets (scoffers) will appear and fool many people. Such will be the spread of evil that many people's love will grow cold.*]

[*Revelation 21:8b - ...and All liars - the place for them is the Lake burning with fire and sulfur which is the second death.*]

In this venue, God is the Creator of All Truth!

An Open and Personal Testimony

This is something I would like to share in this book, a Testimony (Letter) written and sent out through my Outreach Ministry (Ken-na Outreach) in 2018. I had mentioned it earlier in Chapter III as I was explaining The Lake of Fire and Sheol. This is an experience I had when the Lord took me out in Spirit to witness something I believe no one else in this creation has ever witnessed in this detail before. What I witnessed was truly frightening and beyond amazing! I know God has a purpose for everything He does, so I hope this Glorifies God and gives encouragement to the reader; for the day is coming and is already here, when all of those in Christ shall witness what I am mentioning in this letter.

I call this, " **Suddenly it Comes Upon You** ".

*   *   *   *   *   *

My Dearest Brethren, from Ken, who is a Teacher and Elder within the Body of Christ, to spread the Good News and reveal the Truth. May God Bless you all in this reading.

Once again, the Lord has given me something that I must share with you; two great visions that the Lord God has given me. It is something that I was allowed to witness and had a very brief participation in, but with everlasting impact and consequence. I can't give an exact amount of time involvement because this was something that God revealed outside the body, in Spirit, where these events are taking place right now. I am not the first person to ever have such a vision of this or be part of its presentation by God, but I am bound by these two visions to reveal its truth to you all.

When God reveals any part of His Purpose to mankind, the purpose behind it is to give mankind a view and insight into the Will of God, His Will for us, in order that He may be Glorified.

The first part of this vision (I don't know what else to call it), I believe is something that the Lord is revealing to me alone, I have not in the last 44 years of my walk with Christ ever heard anyone speak of this vision before. It was a replay of something God showed me years ago, but this time its impact was so great I could barely contain my senses in front of it.

In the first vision, I was standing in front of two tremendously large double-sided doors. It looked like they were made of cast iron with huge hinges on both sides from top to bottom. As I looked around, it looked like I was in a huge rock cave or cavern underground. Unlike the first time the Lord gave me this vision some years back, I could hear coming from behind the doors a loud thunderous roaring sound. All of a sudden, two large angels appeared standing at both doors ready to open them. Then a voice that sounded like thunder and the doors opened inward. As they opened the sight beyond them was both horrific and tremendous. It looked like an ocean of molten fire, churning like molten metal in a furnace. There was no heat coming from it, but I could sense the strong Presence of God in the midst of it everywhere. I personally had no fear of it and I knew it was not a place that I was going to be entering into. The two angels were standing at the entrance blocking any entry that I could make. My desire was not to enter, but to witness its unbelievable immensity. I knew what it was I was looking at, but as I did the first time the Lord showed it to me, I asked the Lord, "What is this?" The Spirit answered, "*It is the Lake of Fire*". I replied, "the one you revealed to your Apostle?" and the Spirit answered, "*Yes*". Then the Spirit said to me, "*It has been prepared since before the foundations of the earth for Satan and his Fallen Angels. It is The Place of their Holding and Eternal Damnation.*" Then the Spirit reminded me that it is also the Second Death of the Final Judgement of God, for all human beings who are found guilty of Blasphemy against the Word of God and would not receive His Free Gift of Salvation.

As I stood gazing upon this Ocean of Fire, the shear knowledge of what I was gazing upon came to me, it is the Love of God which is this Fire. The Love of God, which is a Burning Fire and will be that substance of their torment forever and ever; as creatures of God's Creation are totally made separated from any part of His Eternal Love and thrown into that Fire of His Love will burn and torment them from within, and without consuming them.

Then a second vision appeared to me; what looked like small individual cubed rooms, about four (4) feet by four (4) feet squared and maybe six feet tall, completely engulfed in darkness, but the darkness was not like here on earth, not like being in a completely dark closet and you couldn't see your hand in front of your face; it was the complete absence of any light, not the covering to shadow or restrict light from coming in, there was no light at all coming from any direction, inside or out. Beside me was an Angel of the Lord, but he did not say a word the whole time, just steadfastly standing beside me. I believe it was the physical Presence of God with me in order that I may survive and withstand being in the presence of this darkness. What the Lord was showing me (telling me) was that on earth (in the physical universe He has Created) the existence of all things comes directly from Him (which is Light) and all sources of Light comes as a direct result of His Presence in all things Created.

Wherever we are in the physical universe, there is light coming from every direction. Even when darkness intrudes on the source of light, there is a consistent radiance existing. We can always come out of the darkness into the light, but in this place, it was spiritual darkness and transparent, I could see through it. It was like looking through a dark bluish glass (crystal clear), with no radiance behind or in front of it. There were individuals (humans) inside these cubed rooms, and they were being inhibited from free form movement inside their space. They were all reacting to an internal (personal) torment, like they were insane and in great anguish, some thrashing around wailing and others holding their heads screaming continuously and beating themselves. I was in close proximity at times to them, and could clearly see them, but they could not see me. I asked the Lord how this was; and The Spirit told me that I was among the living, and these were among the dead. Their torment is the result of their total separation from God. I asked the Lord, how could they be totally separated from God, who made that decision; The Spirit answered me, "*THEY made that decision!*" At that moment, everything shook, and I could see every person falling to their knees trembling in fear. It felt like a double-edged sword had gone through me, then out of me again. It was the Word of God speaking.

The Lord spoke one more thing to me before taking me out of that place; The Spirit revealed what I was witnessing and where this place was; it is the darkness that is inside every human being, the holding place where God has separated the Darkness from the Light. It is the Grave [SHEOL], it is Death, and the captive place of bondage before the Final Day of Judgement (Revelation 20:11-15); and it is more real than anything we have experienced in our human physical life on earth, for it is Eternal.

The Lord made it quite clear that this is not what He intended for Mankind; this is not what His Heart desired for us. This is a willful desire of the individuals here to reject the Free Gift of Salvation that God has provided to every person ever conceived and born. It is the final outcome of their blasphemous and arrogant lives, where now, right at this moment, they are in complete and utter Eternal Darkness and fear and torment; not torment like being hung and having your flesh ripped apart from your body kind of torment, but fear that is so intense and completely incarcerating that it engulfs every molecule of your being. There is no goodness or love or satisfaction of any kind in the midst of the pain and anguish which is being suffered without substance of time, continuous and unceasing with no hope of any end in sight. This is what death has brought onto them, not an end to all things, but the everlasting beginning of unending torment. This is the outcome of complete and total separation from God and the attributes you shared while you were alive in your body as a human being on earth. There is no word in any language that can begin to describe the kind of fear which leads to utter torment like this is.

It must be totally understood that God has completely and everlastingly provided a "way out" to this kind of end for each and every person who has ever been born. God does not send anyone to Eternal Darkness and Damnation; they condemn themselves to it.

God is not a statue or piece of jewelry you wear or icon you have hanging from your rear-view mirror.

God is not a philosophy or religion or good feeling which comes and goes at our pleasure.

God is not everything around us, He is the Creator of all things. There is only One God.

God is not an unseen force that exists throughout the universe and has no interaction with us.

God is Holy, He is the only One who is Holy.

God is Love and God is Spirit.

God is Eternal, He has No Beginning, and He has No End; He was not Created, He is the Creator.

He is the Judge of All of His Creation, He is God!

As the Spirit commands it to be revealed, there is only One God and He has revealed Himself to His Creation as One God: Father, Son and Holy Spirit, One in the Same. He has revealed Himself to all of mankind without exception as the Savior of Mankind; as the Son of God; as the Son of Man; as The Father to His Children who will receive Him as such; as Jesus the Christ (Yeshua ADONAI), The King of Kings and The Lord of Lords.

Make no mistake of it, He is Lord, and He is God!

Rounding up the Truth

I remember my grandfather telling me when I was just a young boy, "A man's word is all he's got, if you can't trust what he says or if he is a liar, then don't do business with him. Anyone who doesn't tell you the Truth is not your friend."

Another one of his infamous sayings was, "If I had a dollar for every time someone told me a lie, I'd be rich".

Life is a Give and Take. The Givers give and the Takers take.

Kind of like the "Dog eat Dog" mentality of a hardened and cold world order where it's 'Every Man for Himself".

My grandfather was born in the late 1800's and came from a time and era when a man gave his word and they shook hands on it, then it was considered a binding contract, legal and court worthy in retribution if broken.

He was raised in an environment where if he told his father a lie, he'd be taken out back to the woodshed and get his behind whooped.

It wasn't considered an act of abuse, but rather a loving and caring father who wanted his son to be an upstanding citizen and trustworthy man.

If you did something wrong you got punished for it and if you did something good, you got rewarded for it, but it was expected that "Good" was the common order of what a person's character should be and being evil and a liar was not.

His father believed that if you spared the rod, you'll spoil the child; and spoiled didn't mean making a brat out of him, it meant to keep him from becoming rotten and criminal.

He would have been 135 years old on his birthday this year (2025) and I know that he would be appalled at the condition of this world today and especially the United States of America.

The current state of this world order has become so attuned to accepting evil as the new form of righteousness and rewriting history to fit into a new political correctness and agenda, that no one being raised as a child today has any clue what "Good" really is, as set by the standard of our past.

Our nation's Constitution and the Rights and Liberty as directed under it are being dissolved without having to rewrite a single word in the Constitution or the Bill of Rights.

Deception through the means of Social and Ethnic Diversity, Greed and Liberal Agendas have enticed factions of perversion and lawlessness within our society to invade the Rule of Law and empower the lawless nature of evil men to persuade change towards Anarchy.

The prayer for the United States of America from this point forward is not for God to Bless America, but rather God Help America!

We have gone way beyond the "Point of No Return" for God's Blessing any longer and are now subject to His Judgment.

Listen! as Believers in Christ, as His Body united (the Church), we are not supposed to be accepting or living under the presence of evil.

The only reason evil has any precedence in the life of a Christian is because they let it!

We are to totally reject the evil thing and supersede it with Faith that resists and fights against it.

We ARE NOT to succumb and let evil have prominence around us or overwhelming presence in front of us.

We are to fight and fight and fight against it with complete and total Faith, without any doubt, that we shall overcome it through what Yeshua has declared "Finished" on the Cross!

Do not let anyone tell you that we are to be passive with evil and that we are not to physically fight against evil things.

When Yeshua said for us to love even your enemy, He didn't mean it in the context for us to embrace the evil of our enemy with hugs and kisses and let them have their way with us; but we are to keep in our hearts the compassion and Love of Christ to pray for their salvation, in that they would come to the conviction of receiving Yeshua as their Lord and Saviour.

If your enemy comes to you with a repentant heart asking for forgiveness, no matter what they may have done to you, you are to receive them with a heart of forgiveness and love. That their act of repentance is your opportunity to show the Love of Christ and pronounce the Gospel to them.

God created man to live in His Presence and have all of the Substance of Truth and Liberty in order to be free; but the sin of Disobedience has bound us to death and requiring substantiation in order to atone for the Sin we have committed against a Holy God.

[Ephesians 1:4 - *Even before the world was made, God had already chosen us to be His through our union with Christ, so that we would be holy and without fault before him.*]

[2Corinthians 3:16-17 - *Nevertheless when one turns to the Lord, the veil is taken away. Now the Lord is the Spirit; and where the Spirit of the Lord is, there is liberty.*]

The Standard for Truth and Righteousness has been given to all of mankind through the "*Word of God*" and the Sacrifice of His death and resurrection.

Did Yeshua go too far with this when He took it to the Cross; when He was whipped and beaten almost to death, afterwards forced to carry His own Cross (estimated to have weighed at least 100 lbs) on top of His blood gushing and shredded flesh to the place of His crucifixion.

Where He was nailed to it through the wrist area of both hands piercing through the Carpal Nerve causing thrusting and burning pain which shot up the Brachial network of nerves to His brain, and then nailed through His feet causing burning agony, then raised up to a vertical position and slammed downward into the placement hole in the ground where His whole body felt the impact of the downward force causing excruciating pain; then hung on that Cross having to support his body weight by upward thrusts pushing on His nail driven feet in order to gasp a breath of air into His lungs, while being cursed, mocked and insulted by the crowd below Him.

Then as He slowly agonized through the painful suffocation by his blood coagulating into thick serum and his heart barely able to circulate it through his body, he takes upon Himself all of the sins of the world and agonizes incomprehensible suffering as sin pierces His Sinless Body and Soul.

He felt and endured all of the immoral, despicable and filthy perversion and sin of every human, in a way that no mortal man could ever withstand, yet He endured.

And even at this, His Life could not be taken from Him, death could not come upon Him.

For six hours he suffered and at the moment that God the Father was satisfied with the fulfillment of His Sin Offering, the Son of God Commanded "*It Is Finished!*"; and He freely gave up His Life and commanded His Spirit to the Father (YaHaVah).

All of this He did as the sacrifice for all of us; when He gave His Life by the shedding of His Blood so that we could be part of the Grace and Mercy of God the Father seeing us blameless and without sin, while He took our sins from us and placed them upon Himself to stand in proxy in our behalf, so that the Father would declare us faultless and only see us through the New Covenant of His Atonement and Propitiation; mankind once again could enter into the Holy Place of His Sanctification and be Face to Face with God.

The sacrifice was so great because the offense is so great.

Sin demands that all of our lives be taken and the outcome is death and the result should be damnation for each and every one of us; but God forbids that outcome by His Grace and affords clemency through His Great Love and Mercy to all who will receive, by Heartfelt Faith, the Eternal Sacrifice that the Son of God gave on behalf of all humanity.

God the Father demanded that a blood sin offering be made for the remission of sin.

This was being done through the Law by the shedding of the Blood of an animal sacrifice, which gave a temporary Atonement, but required it to be performed year after year on the appointed Day of Atonement (Yom Kippur) according to the Law of Moses.

As I said at the beginning of this book, there is no middle ground or gray area within the Truth; anything other than the Truth is a Lie. Truth is a stand-alone and Eternal Entity.

The Death part and shedding of the Blood Sacrifice is only the half of it, this secured all of us our forgiveness from all sin for evermore.

God was satisfied with fulfilling that for all of Eternity, but it did not secure our resurrection from death to life and conquer death forever.

God the Father had to raise Yeshua from death and place Him at the Right Hand of the Power of God in order to conquer death and preserve our Salvation for all of Eternity.

We are saved by the death and resurrection of the Son of God.

Had the Father not raised Yeshua from the grave, then we would have no Salvation for Life Eternal. The Blood would secure the forgiveness of our sins forever, but there would be no salvation to grasp onto.

His resurrection means our resurrection and Eternal Life through the Blood Covenant of His Holy Sacrifice.

He is God, One with the Father, and the Spirit
(ELOHIM)

The Bottom-Line

This book is not meant to be a best seller or written for world acclaim or the advent of a Pastoral or Evangelical fame and notoriety.

It has been over a year in the writing and a very heart-felt and soul-searching endeavor to make sure I was extenuating the voice of the Spirit and under the Perfect Will of God in writing this.

This book has been inspired by the Word of God and manifested through the Holy Spirit as a testimony to the Truth.

Even as short in content as it is, it is exactly what God is wanting to say through His servant and He has told me that it will be used greatly after that Man of Sin (Anti-Christ) hits the stage; a lot of people will be searching for the truth then and many will come to Christ through the witness of what we leave behind now!

There is righteous anger which can be expressed through a Child of God and be in tune to the Spirit of God and the Truth which is expelled through the Spirit and expressed from a human venue.

We can express ourselves in plain human language and vernacular and not have to act with a false holiness and politically correctness in how we express it in order to conform to what some religious preponderance or dogma expects of us.

I mean, God forbid if we convict any of those Religious Zealots who act all holier-than-thou, all clothed in self-righteousness, all clean on the outside, with wonderful speech and saying exactly what itchy ears are wanting to hear but inside are full of corruption and dead man's bones. Deceivers of the Faith and devils in disguise.

In too many instances throughout the Church Age, the Religious Zealots and Church Bureaucrats have dominated the message and stifled the freedom and movement of the Spirit to work in the Church Assembly and dictate the fellowship.

Because of this, many never find their salvation through Christ and only have a religious experience and membership in a church organization; God knows how they put their time in going to Sunday Service week after week and slipping a couple of bucks in the Offering Basket.

Most leave the building as empty and expressionless as when they walked in.

As the Scripture says, "*No one mocks God...and nothing comes back to Him Void!*"

The bottom-line is that God knows your heart, whether you confess Him or reject Him.

No one makes a fool of God! His Will shall be done on earth as it is in Heaven.

There is no looking back or repentance in Eternity Forever!

There is no forgiveness or salvation or second chances in Eternity Forever!

There is no debating what the Truth is, there is no time or purgatory or the ability to Right any Wrongs in Eternity Forever!

This is all available to us <u>NOW</u> in this life, once we pass through the portal of death the outcome of your Eternity Forever is sealed, your ability to change anything <u>ends</u>!

Eternity can occur at any moment for any of us.
It's <u>your</u> decision where you spend it!

Yeshua is Lord and God!

(1John 5:19-20)

Kenna Publications © 2014, 2022, 2025

www.ingramcontent.com/pod-product-compliance
Lightning Source LLC
Chambersburg PA
CBHW062039290426
44109CB00026B/2669